The London Dungeon Book of Crime and Punishment

The London Dungeon Book of Crime and Punishment

RICHARD BYRNE

LITTLE, BROWN AND COMPANY

DEDICATION

To Leah, Patrick and Bunty
and for David Bodilly,
Don Clarke and Jimmy Lindie

A *Little, Brown* Book

First published in Great Britain in 1993
by Little, Brown and Company

A CIP catalogue record for this book
is available from the British Library.

Designed and typeset by
Vivitext Creative Services

Printed and bound in Great Britain
by Butler & Tanner, Frome.

ISBN 0 316 90351 5

Little, Brown and Company (UK) Limited
165 Great Dover Street
London SE1 4YA

CONTENTS

v

INTRODUCTION

London has been a cruel city. In displays of public torment it has put to death tens of thousands of its sons and daughters, and the prisoners it chose not to kill have been whipped through the streets, branded and mutilated, thrown into foul gaols, and transported across the face of the earth to labour and to perish.

Londoners may no longer line the road from the prison to the gallows, or run from their homes to gather around the pillory, but no city is so fascinated by its crimes, its criminals, and its punishments. Good deeds and great kings go unremembered, but the stories of murder and treason, hangmen and headsmen, are told again and again: London takes a pride in lawlessness, relishes every grisly detail.

In truth, the history of crime is among the richest sources of comment on the lives of both kings and common people. Because crime and punishment are always news, they have been remembered and recorded in great depth and detail, by every degree of observer from gutter journalists to Pepys and Boswell and Dickens.

We are lucky. These are sheltered times for London, safe from great plagues and untouched by great violence for nearly fifty years. It will do us no harm to remember that we have no special claim to enlightenment – for centuries our city was notorious for its extraordinary appetite for public killing and its indifference to suffering. History is more than rich pageantry and tales of great heroes – at The London Dungeon, and in this book, you will glimpse the life in the shadows, the fate of the villains.

PART
1

Metropolitan Life, Capital Crimes

Lᴏndon did not grow from a single centre, like the trunk of a tree, but from three original settlements. Much the largest was the City of London, founded by the Romans on a site already much used as a harbour and trading place – a great city which had reached fully 50,000 people at its colonial peak. Across the Thames lay a long sprawl of riverside wharves, taverns, and market gardens – this was Southwark, developed by the Danes. Upstream on the north bank was Westminster, at first just an island of firm ground surrounded by marsh, chosen by the later Anglo-Saxon kings for their court. The City, though so much larger than its neighbours, was constrained at first by its walls, within which the population built upwards and inwards. All these settlements were to grow like inkblots swamping villages and hamlets around and between them, until they merged into the great and smoky Victorian capital.

London grew because every famine and misfortune drove families off the land, along the roads to the capital; after every war, soldiers who could not go home were drawn to London. In times of plenty, bright young men came to make honest fortunes, and their rascal cousins fled local scandal to find a bolthole in the big city where no one knew their name. Long before there were dry roads or railways, ordinary people made their way slowly along waterlogged or dusty roads to deliver produce and livestock, to bring and buy goods and tools.

All came because the vastness of London made it the biggest consumer, and its docks and markets were the greatest exchange, the place where profits and plunder could be found. Down all the centuries of London's criminal history two traditional figures appear again and again: the eternal victim was the out-of-towner with pockets full of cash, the gullible country chicken ready to be plucked by force or by guile. His fellow traveller was the bold young man, the eager underworld recruit ready to risk the rope for a fancy suit and a roaring reputation.

The London of thousands

The City was always an anthill, building up and out. No street map could ever show the extraordinary tangle of alleys and passages, of shacks and sheds and stables and stores in which the people lived. Londoners crammed themselves under every available roof, raised crude shelters instead of stout houses. In every generation there were speculators who set out to build homes for the prosperous, only to find that there was more money to be made by letting each house to a dozen poorer families.

London was too small for the classes to live apart. For as long as they stayed within its walls, the rich had no immunity to the dangers of City life, and when the disease and the clamour and the crime became intolerable, the wealthy simply left town. The power and wealth of the nobility had always lain in their country estates, and to be close to the court at Westminster they built fine palaces and town houses, like the Somerset House of the 1550s, along the Strand and beyond. The princes of trade bought estates in Middlesex and Essex to create the original stockbroker belt; City houses were still a necessity, but as places of business rather than full-time residences: these were the first office buildings.

Even as it grew to be the greatest trading centre in the world, London kept the habits and customs of a market town: meeting in taverns and coffee houses, merchants sealed deals with a handshake, relying on reputation and trust for their security. This taste for life on a small scale was built into the very shape of the City: when the Great Fire laid waste to the City in 1666, every plan for grand reconstruction was rejected. Though Peter the Great would design St Petersburg and Louis XIV would create a new Paris, Londoners wanted their old familiar narrow streets and alleys, and like the weeds that would smother the bomb sites of the Blitz, the ancient winding ways grew again across the ruins.

Crime was simple, too. Robbery was easy in those tight unlit alleys, and the trusting out-of-towner who mixed drinking with business was easy prey for a swindler blessed with an honest face. A police force, like grand planning, was still a foreign idea to be distrusted, and London's crooks had no fear of the elderly watchmen on their slack patrols.

When fear of capture was unlikely to deter criminals, the authorities put great faith in the effects of brutal public punishment, but this too was an idea more fitted to the village than a great capital. The scenes at the stocks and the pillory could be contained, but the sombre spectacle of parading criminals to the gallows, intended to inspire fear and respect for the law, became instead a grotesque carnival.

In the larger London, public killing was too common to evoke terror, and attracted crowds too vast to be controlled. For a hanging, Londoners in their tens of thousands left their homes and their work to join in a drunken and riotous public holiday, toasting great villains as proud heroes. When there was no hanging to watch, sensation-seekers had long been able to tip the keeper to see the condemned in their wards at Newgate, from the sixteenth century they could buy their way into Bridewell to watch floggings, and a hundred years later they found great sport in watching the chained and caged patients suffer in Bedlam.

The first million

London housed more than a million people before Waterloo, and between the poor and the prosperous a new class had grown. By 1815 London had expanded across and beyond the old centres, and in the distinctive new flat-fronted houses lived the clerks and managers, the shopkeepers and professionals needed in the capital of the world's first industrial nation. These new middle-class households had servants who lived in, but also needed the day labour of a much larger army of working poor. Behind the vast mansions of the nobility, between the town houses of the merchants and professional men, lived the bootblacks, the street sweepers, the delivery men, the washerwomen. Families lived above the horses in the mews, in lean-tos and outbuildings, in the rooms above shops and the cellars beneath them.

In these early years of the nineteenth century, attitudes to crime and criminals went through their greatest changes. The belief began to grow that criminals might be reformed by prisons devised to correct as well as punish; though hanging was still prescribed by law for more than two hundred crimes, judges and juries became increasingly reluctant to demand death for petty offences; at last, Londoners were prepared to contemplate the creation of a regular police force. Simple Non-conformist religious beliefs and a secular reliance on rational solutions to human problems both grew with industrialisation, and both demanded new explanations for criminal behaviour and new approaches to punishment.

The London of many millions

In the 1840s, soon after the completion of the new Houses of Parliament, the population of inner London passed two million, and it would double again by the end of the century. The outer suburbs – Barnet to Croydon, Uxbridge to Ilford – followed, until they housed a further four million. London had become not only the capital of a nation, but the centre of the broadest empire in history and the largest city in the world.

It was the lower middle class, and fresh drafts of skilled working men, who now stretched the boundaries of London. When all the miles and miles of familiar Victorian terraces were built in the suburbs for the middle-class battalions of clerks and their servants, they filled open land which had seemed very distant just a generation before but was now made close by the railways. It was the railways themselves, the Post Office, and the other providers of lifetime employment, which supported the growth of a skilled and respectable working class.

This was the London of Jack the Ripper and Sherlock Holmes, a foggy melée of handcarts and horse-trams, where the traditional underworld still thrived, and high society still fought to suppress its scandals, but where respectable privacy seemed to conceal new and secret evils. There were police on the streets to suppress vice and violence, but in their Gothic villas, behind net curtains, suburban poisoners and smartly dressed swindlers were discovered by the new detectives. This was a society in which propriety mattered, and after trials more elaborate and formal than any before, criminals would disappear for years into the new prisons, or die on scaffolds now hidden from view.

THE TOWER OF LONDON

The most famous of all London's buildings, visited by millions every year, will never again be a royal palace nor a military stronghold. Following a Yeoman Warder on a guided tour, it is tempting to regard

the Tower as a grand relic, no more than a decorative museum and a fine backdrop for family photographs.

Never forget that the Tower is still what it has been since the days of William the Conqueror – an official state prison, within which enemies of the Crown have been locked up and executed for all nine centuries of its history. When there is a threat to the realm, the gates are closed to visitors, the guards mustered, and the cells prepared.

THE WHITE TOWER
This is the original fortress built by William the Conqueror to dominate London, built of stone shipped from France. Important captives were lodged in fine apartments, but the cellars of the White Tower were a gaol for the most wretched prisoners, and the home of the rack.

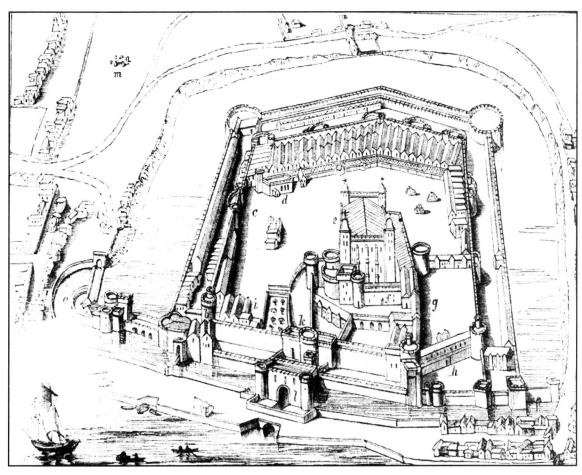

In most towns, the castle is a centrepiece around which houses huddle for protection, the last shelter for the people in the face of attack or siege. But when William I came to conquer London, it was a trading centre with no fortress. He built the Tower not to protect the capital but to dominate it, and for nine hundred years it has been the sovereign's stronghold and the greatest of the state prisons.

Later kings circled William's original keep – the tall square central White Tower – with extra walls and towers, to become the home not only of the royal servants but of a large garrison of troops, gangs of shipwrights, workers in the Royal Mint and the Armoury, and every kind of specialist from astronomers to zoo-keepers. It was a crowded, busy, noisy, place.

It was this loyal garrison, as much as the thick walls, which made the Tower an effective prison, and from the earliest times those whom the Crown chose as enemies were brought here. Modern tour guides remind

THE TOWER
The Tower of London when it was still surrounded by a full moat, with the scaffold of Tower Hill visible in the top left hand corner. Each one of the outer towers served as a prison at one time, and in this view it is easy to see how the river entrance – Traitor's Gate – provided the most secure access to the fortress.

us of the royal and noble captives, but there were nameless hundreds more: prisoners of every war – French, Dutch, Spanish, American and German; oppressed Jews; English rebels and traitors; Irish, Welsh and Scots patriots; religious opponents of the Crown; military mutineers.

Of the 1758 recorded prisoners, we know that a rare few prisoners of rank were lodged in comfort, allowed to retain their servants and enjoy the company of their families, but the rest were stowed away down in cellars and storerooms, and high in the towers.

Medieval prisoners

The first prisoner for whom we have a name was Ranulf Flambard, Bishop of Durham, who fell foul of the King because he refused to accept a lay court's jurisdiction. He is also the first known escaper: he arranged for a rope to be smuggled to him, and on 2 February 1106 got his guards drunk, and climbed down to freedom. He was luckier than a Welshman called Gruffyd in the next century, whose rope of torn blankets parted and sent him to his death.

Of all the atrocities committed in the Tower none was so vile as the callous exploitation of Jews. The Jews had been encouraged to come to London by the Norman kings, and the community was twice taken into the tower for safety when feelings against foreigners ran high, but they were also several times detained for ransom. In an attempt to boost his own popularity, in 1278 Edward I imprisoned six hundred Jews on false charges of coin-clipping – 260 were hanged, and most of the rest died of ill-treatment and neglect, probably in the lowest levels of the White Tower.

The long wars with France brought drafts of prisoners – three hundred citizens of Caen were carried there, and after each great battle, soldiers, nobles and royalty were held captive until their ransoms were paid. Accommodation was strictly according to rank: King John II of France, captured at Poitiers in 1356, was permitted to live in luxury high in the White Tower. For three years he held court surrounded by his entourage of courtiers and servants, cooks and guards while the money was raised for his ransom. The Tower proved safer for John than for English kings: Henry VI was murdered in 1471 while at prayer in the Wakefield Tower, and the boy King, Edward V, was put to death with his younger brother the Duke of York in 1483, on the orders of Richard III. These were the famous Princes in the Tower, and the part of the fortress in which they were murdered lost its old title of the Garden Tower to become forever the Bloody Tower. The controversy about the princes' deaths is still lively, but it seems probable that two skeletons found in the seventeenth century and exhumed once more in 1933 for thorough examination, are indeed those of the murdered boys.

It was in the sixteenth century that the Tower received its most famous prisoners, victims of the struggles for power and the religious conflicts of the Tudor dynasty. When Henry VIII came to the throne, the Tower was still the principal home of the royal court – he redecorated the palace within the Tower for the coronation of his second wife, Anne Boleyn, then sent her to imprisonment, trial and death there. By the end of his reign he had abandoned it for Whitehall Palace. The Tower became a grand prison, used time and again to hold the king's enemies, and a private place of execution for those who offended him. In every time of tension or war since then the Tower has received fresh prisoners. Elizabeth, Henry's daughter by Anne, was imprisoned by her half-sister Mary for three months, but survived to succeed her. Sir Walter Raleigh spent a total of fourteen years there, making a home with his family and servants, and allowed to use a henhouse as a makeshift laboratory: he used his time to write a history of the world.

Samuel Pepys was held briefly in 1679, accused by the perjurer Titus Oates of giving naval secrets to the French, but he was bailed and later able to clear his name.

Judge Jeffreys was taken into protective custody there, and the eighteenth-century agitators John Wilkes and Lord George Gordon each spent time behind its walls. The Cato Street Conspirators were lodged there briefly on the way to common prison cells; Sir Roger Casement was held in the Tower before his trial, and Hitler's deputy Rudolf Hess came to the Tower for four days after parachuting into Scotland on his deluded peace mission.

In the Outer Ward, the space between the walls on the western side, are chambers let into the wall itself, and it is these which were used as a military headquarters to which captured enemies, such as downed airmen and captured naval crews, could be brought for questioning and brief detention.

Nearby is the covered small arms range where spies convicted by courts martial faced firing squads. Eleven were executed in the First World War, but just one man, a German officer called Josef Jakobs, in the Second. He was taken from Wandsworth prison, where he had impressed the governor with his calm dignity, on the morning of 15 August 1941, and at the Tower tied to a simple chair to be shot. It would be comforting to hope that Jakobs will be the last of the many to be put to death within the Tower, but the Tower is more than just a time-worn tourist attraction – it remains officially a prison, always ready for use.

Tower Green

The Green, an open space within the Tower, provided a discreet place of execution for those whom the King had condemned, but preferred not to display at Tyburn or even outside the walls on Tower Hill.

The first to die here was the Duke of Hastings, who had been invited to dinner in 1483 by Richard III (when he was Protector to the young Edward V), but seized and taken out onto the Green to be crudely beheaded on a convenient baulk of timber.

Henry VIII ordered three beheadings on Tower Green. His second wife, Anne Boleyn, was condemned for adultery, and chose to be executed with a sword rather than an axe, by a headsman brought from France for the task in 1536. No block was used: when she knelt to pray and was blindfolded, the executioner crept up, drew the sword from under a pile of straw, and beheaded her with a single stroke.

The Countess of Salisbury was condemned by Henry VIII for treason without trial or confession. She was seventy-one years old in 1541 when she was led onto the Green, but defiantly declared her innocence, refused to kneel to the block, and told the executioner 'if he would have her head, to get it off as best he could; so that he was constrained to fetch it off slovenly.'

Catherine Howard, Henry's fifth wife, was put to death on Tower Green in 1542, having asked that the block be brought to her the night before so that she might practise laying her neck upon it. On the scaffold she said 'If I had married the man I love instead of being dazzled with ambition all would have been well. I die a Queen but I would rather have died the wife of Culpepper.' On her way to the Tower she had seen the heads of her lovers Culpepper and Dereham displayed on London Bridge.

Lady Jane Grey, Queen of England for just nine days, had been elevated to the throne as the puppet of the Duke of Northumberland, but the people preferred Mary Tudor, who replaced her and then ordered her execution to remove her rival once and for all.

Lady Jane was fearful that she might be struck before she had lowered her head to the block, and the headsman reassured her, but once blindfolded she could not find the block with her hands and had to be guided to it by one of her attendants. She was seventeen when she died in 1554.

Robert Devereux, Earl of Essex, once the favourite of Elizabeth I, had recklessly entered into a conspiracy to kidnap and depose her, in order to seize power for himself. On the morning of 25 February 1601, he was led from what is now called the Devereux Tower, and beheaded with three blows of the axe.

The very last to die on Tower Green were not nobles or royalty but three soldiers of Lord Sempill's Regiment (later to become the Black Watch) who were shot in 1743 for taking part in a peaceful protest against poor leadership and treatment. There was great sympathy for them, and the execution was carried out with elaborate concern. As they knelt blindfolded on a plank laid close to the wall of the Chapel, a firing squad moved silently out from cover, weapons ready cocked so as to make no alarming noise, to deliver the final volley.

Tower Hill

The Normans had cleared all cover from the high ground north of the Tower as part of the defences, but the hill was a convenient patch of open land close to the City and it soon became a dump for every kind of waste and filth.

In the troubled reign of Richard II it gained a more sinister status. First, Wat Tyler's men, having seized the Tower, dragged the Archbishop of Canterbury out onto the Hill and crudely chopped off his head using a log as a block. Then powerful nobles compelled the execution of Sir Simon Burley, the king's tutor and close confidant; when Richard overcame the nobles, he ordered that one of their leaders be put to death on the spot where Burley had perished. Tower Hill had become a royal place of execution, where traitors would be punished. It was a convenient site, to which prisoners could be taken without the lengthy, risky, riotous progress to Tyburn: the Tower was royal property, and the Constable of the Tower had a garrison to supervise executions. When a permanent scaffold was erected in the reign of Edward IV, the City authorities protested that they would see no profit from any royal events and as a compromise which satisfied both protocol and commercial interests, the scaffold and the supervision of executions were handed over to the City sheriffs. By custom, Tower Hill became the place for beheading the nobility and the great – Sir Thomas More in 1535, Thomas Cromwell in 1540, the Dukes of Somerset in 1552 and Northumberland in 1553, Archbishop Laud in 1645 and the rebel Duke of Monmouth in 1685 – while their social inferiors were less honourably hanged at Tyburn. One seventeenth-century traitor, a knight rather than a noble, threatened to betray his accomplices until they arranged that he should go to Tower Hill – this satisfied his vanity and he went to his death without naming them.

THE REBEL SCOTTISH LORDS EXECUTED ON TOWER HILL
Hanging at Tyburn was a death for commoners. Prisoners of high rank and degree – usually enemies of the Crown – were beheaded on Tower Hill in spectacles elaborately stage-managed to trumpet their defeat. Troops were drafted in to control crowds and deter unrest; tall grandstands were built to give crowds a clear view; and prisoners were brought from the Tower in a ceremonial procession. This picture shows the execution of the last of the Scottish patriots who had supported the Young Pretender.

The last man to die by the axe in England was beheaded at the Tower. Lord Lovat, a Jacobite plotter captured after the rebellion of 1745, was an old man of eighty with a lifetime of cynical conspiracy behind him. He had rehearsed what he must do on the scaffold with a Yeoman Warder, but when he was led out onto the Hill there were tens of thousands of spectators crammed into the seats of enormous grandstands, which collapsed under the weight, killing at least twenty. Lovat's reaction was wry: 'The more mischief, the more sport!'

TORTURE

It has been common enough for prisoners to suffer beatings from their fellows or cruel loading with irons by their gaolers, but there is one place which is associated with the regular and systematic infliction of purposeful pain – the Tower of London.

Down the centuries the English have had a grisly reputation for punishing their criminals – we have executed extraordinary numbers of minor criminals, and our neighbours are still startled by the length of prison sentences passed in our courts and the squalor in which we keep so many of our prisoners.

This appetite for punishment makes it the more remarkable that we have made use of torture sparingly. There have been many sentences passed which were intended to cause pain, from flogging to the quartering of traitors, yet we have rarely used torture – that is, pain to make an offender confess, or to force him to name other criminals. The reasons do not lie in any compassion of courts or gaolers, but in an early decision to rely on trial by jury. The old ways of deciding guilt in criminal cases had required trial either by battle or by ordeal, and of these the use of ordeal was much more flexible and common, since many defendants, such as women, could not go to battle. Then in 1215, at the Lateran Council, the Church put an end to trial by ordeal, and new ways of resolving cases had to be found.

Some countries chose a judicial system which relied upon gaining a confession from the accused, and created systems of routine torture to make sure of obtaining admissions of guilt. In England the choice was to take the old practice of inviting panels of local people to assist the court, and adapt and develop it into a system of jury trial.

This choice came at a time when kings were trying to unify the laws and courts of England under their own control, partly to protect the people from arbitrary local oppression, but mainly to give the Crown full control across the entire country. The new common law of the king's courts forbade all use of torture, and ordinary offenders were safe from the everyday brutalities inflicted elsewhere. However, the new system also included specialised courts which were not bound by common law, but were controlled by the Crown and in effect made their own law. Thus the power to inflict pain was reserved to the Crown and the Privy Council, to be used in cases where the interests of the state, or the dignity of the monarch were at stake.

In the twelfth century, Henry II ordered the use of torture to extract

THE RACK
Though muscular torturers are shown applying stretching the poor victim, it was more common for the questioners to be left alone with their captive: they usually wanted to extract secrets which were not for the ears of others.

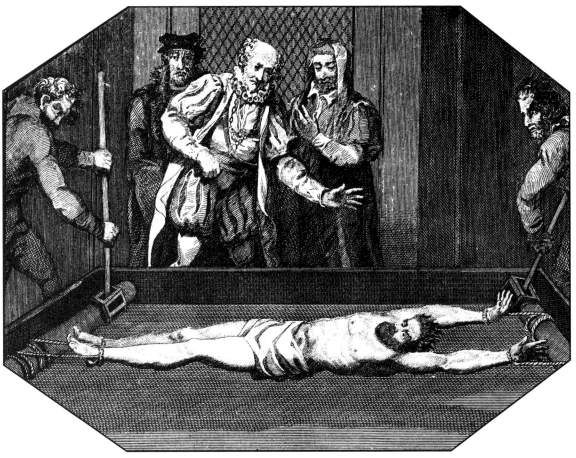

discrediting confessions from the Knights Templar, a religious order believed to be corrupt and heretical. The methods were probably simple and brutal, but we are told that several of the knights were confined in a small cell called Little Ease, which was lightless and dank, and too small to permit standing or lying at full length. This is a variety of torment much used in our own time, now given the grander title of sensory deprivation, and known to be effective.

There is just one period in our history when the authorities were so afraid of treachery, when religious and national conflicts were so dangerous, that torture became commonplace. These were two sinister centuries during which the Tower of London in particular became notorious for the agonies inflicted on rebels and plotters, priests and those regarded as heretics by one faith or the other. Prisoners in the Tower could be tortured in any place convenient to their gaolers – many of the instruments used were portable and could be taken to the prisoner's own cell, or employed in the torturer's home – but the lowest floor of the old White Tower was certainly a torture chamber of the kind seen in horror films. One Jesuit recalled that 'The chamber was underground and dark, particularly near the entrance. It was a vast, shadowy place and every device and instrument of human torture was there.'

The custom was to display the tools of torture to each victim as a preliminary. This matter-of-fact tour of the pain-inflicting devices was intended to soften resolve and loosen tongues: some prisoners must have been so terrified as to confess immediately, and even the bravest and most steadfast knew that torment and death were now inevitable.

Since the purpose of torture was to aid interrogation, it was supervised and controlled by the officials who were to ask the questions; in many cases, a simple instruction was given to the Lieutenant of the Tower, the supervisor of the warders, to torture named prisoners and report what they had said. For the most important prisoners, high officers of state conducted the questioning – Guy Fawkes was interrogated by the Secretary of State, the Lord Privy Seal and the Lord High Admiral – and from time to time even kings themselves might take part.

The tortures themselves ranged from the crude and simple – beating and the application of hot irons – to the use of elaborate machinery. Most famous and most dreaded was the rack, an instrument imported from the Continent in 1420 by the Duke of Exeter when he was

Constable of the Tower, and known wryly as 'the Duke of Exeter's daughter'. The oak frame of the rack stood on legs about three feet tall, and its victims were first laid beneath it, to be raised and then stretched by ropes attached to their wrists and ankles. Extra traction was applied by levers and held by ratchets, to pull upon the joints at the shoulders and hips, elbows and knees. Racking was a torment which could be finely controlled to achieve each required level of pain, from the first bite of the ropes to the ruin of the body by dislocation. A resistant prisoner would be brought to the rack again and again: the inevitability of greater pain drained the victim's mental strength during the pauses as surely as the rack itself crippled his body.

Guy Fawkes, the most famous man to suffer on the rack, refused to name his accomplices in the Gunpowder Plot, and King James himself ordered that 'if he will no other ways confess, the gentler tortures are to be first used unto him ...'; after a half-hour on the rack Fawkes began to talk, and then was stretched until his hips and shoulder joints were parted. At that point, 'told he must come to it again and again, from day to day', he gave his interrogators everything they needed. The details of the plot, the names of the conspirators, were all written down in the confession which he could barely sign, the document which enabled the king's men to round up and exterminate so many.

As cruel as the rack was, there was another apparatus which worked in quite the opposite way. Sir Leonard Skeffington became Lieutenant of the Tower in 1534, and having studied the rack closely he invented a monstrous clamp which would fold and press the body upon itself, and which had the advantage of being easily dismantled and portable enough to carry to any room or cell in the castle. Victims of this new device – known of course as Skeffington's Daughter – knelt within a framework which 'holds the body in a threefold manner, the lower legs being pressed to the thighs, the thighs to the belly, and thus both are locked with two iron clamps ... the whole body is so bent that with some the blood exudes from the tips of the hands and feet; with others the box of the chest being burst, a quantity of blood is expelled from the mouth and nostrils.'

Each large device had its smaller counterparts: prisoners could be stretched by suspending them by the wrists and attaching weights to their ankles; Skeffington's invention was the largest of a great assortment of other clamps used to crush the feet, the legs, the fingers and thumbs. It was easy enough to inflict simple pain by mutilation, pulling teeth and nails, but determined interrogators were better served by methods designed to inflict pain on a body rather than destroy it.

It seems that the official ending of torture owed much to the quick wits of a single man. In 1628 John Felton, who had assassinated the Duke of Buckingham, was interrogated in the Tower by the Bishop of London and the Earl of Dorset. They wanted to know if Felton had accomplices, but he insisted that he had acted quite alone. They threatened him with the rack, but the cool Felton pointed out that torture was against the law, and added with mischief 'If I be put upon the rack I will accuse you, my Lord Dorset, and none but yourself.'

It worked. The bishop told King Charles I, who chose for once not to rely upon royal privilege, but referred the matter to a commission. The commissioners found that 'Felton ought not by the law to be tortured by the rack, for no such punishment is known or allowed by our law.' Having asked for a judgement on the matter Charles had to abide by this finding, and although Felton was hanged for his crime (and one or two men may subsequently have been discreetly racked) torture was officially abolished.

THE MOB

> *What began with a rumour, a street-corner argument, a single angry speech, could swiftly become a public rage spreading faster than fire across London.*

The common people had no vote and no way of making their voices heard by the king or his ministers. Whenever rage, despair or fear overtook them, Londoners would arm themselves with crude weapons and mass in the streets to shout their protests.

The wrath of the mob was very different from the political anger of rebels such as Wat Tyler or Jack Cade, and grievances were usually local; most riots were spontaneous, almost casual. If a local fight got out of hand, or an alarmist rumour reached a neighbourhood, hundreds might gather and rampage through a market or a busy street, tossing goods, breaking windows, and brawling with anyone who stood in their way. Within a couple of hours, perhaps at the first sign of official anger, the mob would dissolve, leaving nothing worse than a few wrecked shops and a few injured bystanders. Deaths were quite rare in these minor outbreaks, and once the damage had been repaired, the outcome was no more than a useful relief to tensions and resentments in the community.

The rioters themselves were usually young men. Notoriously quick to fight were the relatively respectable apprentices, and they would be joined by young nobles and squires – the sons of the rich, young men of good family – and their servants. Tradespeople guarded their privileges: if they thought rivals, particularly foreign merchants, were being favoured, the guilds and companies would seize makeshift weapons and take to the streets to settle the matter.

The authorities were always alarmed by public violence, but had very few men under their command, and for as long as there was no underlying political purpose, they often found it easiest simply to wait and hope that the smaller outbreaks would end as spontaneously as they had begun.

THE GORDON RIOTS –
THE BURNING OF
NEWGATE IN 1780
*Gaols had been always a
target for rioters and rebels,
and this last great attack on
Newgate came during the
anti-Catholic riots of 1780,
burning it just a year after
the prison had been
completely rebuilt.*

Two changes in mob behaviour followed the deposing of James II and the arrival on the throne of William. One came from the new popularity of gin and other spirits: strong drink did more than inflame individuals, it fuelled gang violence. Throughout the eighteenth century, Londoners were terrorised by loutish gangs – The Mohocks, The Bold Bucks and others – who took pleasure in tormenting passers-by, subjecting them to vicious assaults and rapes, capable of killing without provocation. These were young men of good family, beyond control or retribution, often choosing servants and the poor as their victims. Few of the ancient watchmen cared to take the risk of challenging or arresting them, and few magistrates were willing to convict or sentence severely the wayward children of their own class.

More alarming to the authorities was the spirit of Jacobitism – the loyalty to the Stuarts among Scots, Irish and Catholics, and the longing for the return of the exiled Pretender. There were several serious riots by Jacobite sympathisers, and as many anti-Stuart disturbances. To those in power, any public protest carried the threat of a broader attack. In 1715 the great rising prompted the passing of the Riot Act, which ordered the death penalty for rioters and gave magistrates power to summon the military if necessary.

ATTACKING A CHARLEY
Londoners distrusted and despised officers of the law. Young men of every class, from coarse apprentices to wealthy bucks, missed no chance to mock and torment the watchmen.

There was no general rising, and for a generation the Riot Act was little needed or used, but during the second half of the eighteenth century London saw a steady increase in public disorder. There were smaller disturbances: an attack on brothels by sailors, a rampage through the theatres, but two series of major public battles followed: the confrontation with supporters of Wilkes, and a new variety of organised industrial upheaval.

John Wilkes was an outspoken politician, a libertine and a libertarian – 'a blasphemer of his God and libeller of his King' – who had been pilloried and sent to the Tower for writings which offended the government. Hated by the Establishment, Wilkes was a hero to the

COLDBATH FIELDS RIOT
This was the showdown for the London Mob, and the first great test of the Metropolitan Police. During the riot, a policeman was killed, but his colleagues were more disciplined and restrained than their critics had predicted; public sympathy swung to the police.

people, and when in 1770 attempts were made to prevent him from taking the seat in Parliament to which he had been elected, the mob attacked the King's Bench prison to free him, soldiers opened fire, and many were killed and injured.

Unrest among working people had spread through the provinces as the changes of the Industrial Revolution threatened old crafts with new machines, and created harsh privation. Though the capital was generally more prosperous and less desperate, workers from old trades in London took to the streets in organised protest, and were met with great force. In dreadful retribution against coal-heavers – the men who unloaded the capital's supplies from ships and lighters – who had fought the military, seven of their number were taken to Stepney to be hanged before a crowd of fifty thousand.

Organised political protests would continue, but the old-style mob showed its strength in one last great outburst of raw popular anger and prejudice – the Gordon Riots of 1780. Lord George Gordon was eccentric to the point of insanity, and fanatically anti-Catholic. As a step on the way to religious tolerance, Parliament had passed the Catholic Relief Act, but Gordon inflamed a meeting of the Protestant Association, who voted to march on the House of Commons and demand the Act's repeal.

The next day tens of thousands of Londoners rallied in Southwark, the religious fires fuelled by wider frustrations with the king and the government, and to a general cry of 'No Popery!' set out to petition Parliament. It was a Friday, and when Members postponed consideration of the papers until the following week, the angry mob went on a rampage which lasted a week: Catholic houses, shops and chapels were attacked and Newgate prison was burned. The Lord Mayor – John Wilkes, freed by the mob himself just a decade before – led a military defence of the Bank of England. By the time order was restored, more than 450 people had been killed or gravely injured, and although Gordon himself was acquitted of treason, twenty-five of his followers were sentenced to death, including four women.

Governments were quick to grow panicky at any public protest for at least two more generations, but the primitive rage of the mob was never so aroused again. There were outrages in the provinces, but in London a relative prosperity, political reforms, and the use of disciplined police rather than a frightened, rapidly mustered militia, all helped to lower the temperature of later political and industrial protests.

THE UNDERWORLD

'Whoever indeed considers the Cities of London and Westminster, with the late vast Additions of their Suburbs; the great Irregularity of their Buildings, the immense Number of Lanes, Alleys, Courts and Bye-places; must think that, had they been intended for the very Purpose of Concealment, they could scarce have been better contrived. Upon such a View, the whole appears as a vast Wood or Forest, in which a Thief may harbour with as great Security, as Wild Beasts do in the desarts of Africa or Arabia.'
Henry Fielding (1751)

Across London there were dangerous and hidden districts, the homes of thieves and killers, the factories of crime, playgrounds and academies for fresh generations of criminals.

The idea of an underworld is no more than fanciful today: we use the word to describe a loose association of professional criminals. If we describe a man in our newspapers as 'a well-known underworld figure', we are probably pointing to a man who lives comfortably with his family behind a tidy suburban lawn, uses a legitimate occupation as a cover for occasional major crimes, and likes to spend his evenings up West in fashionable clubs.

Once there was an underworld in an older sense, a hell on earth. It had a life in those secretive places where the thieves lived, the robbers slept, and the highwaymen took lodgings, in secret alleys of flophouses and taverns where a fugitive could put himself beyond the reach of the law. A deserter from the army, a pickpocket still clutching a stolen purse, a fraud on the run from his angry victims – if they were strong enough, or cunning enough, any of these could run into the sanctuary of an Alsatia or a St Giles, where no questions would be asked, where the door would slam in the face of a nosy pursuer, and a whole street rise in arms to beat off an intrusion by the constables. Here the honest citizen was in peril not only at night, but at noon. Even where the buildings had once been noble or elegant, generations of criminals had extended and adapted them with cunning. From a window to a gallery, to an alley, to a back door, to a trapdoor, through a roofspace into a crowded bar to a cellar fully three streets away, a man might make his escape. His pursuers would be obstructed or attacked at every step, by loyal neighbours and drunken strangers.

The underworld was more than a word or a concept. It was visible, if only from beyond; in it people were conceived and were born, lived short lives and died.

Shakespeare's underworld – Southwark

> 'Do not associate with the crowds of pimps; do not mingle with throngs in the eating houses; avoid the dicing and the gambling and the theatre and the taverns ... the number of parasites is infinite. Actors, jesters, smooth-skinned lads, Moors, flatterers, pretty-boys, effeminates, paederasts, singing and dancing girls, belly dancers, quacks, sorceresses, extortioners, magicians, night-wanderers, mimes, beggars and buffoons – all this tribe fill the houses.'

This was the advice offered by a monk in Southwark to a visitor, a catalogue of just some of the commercial and fleshly temptations for which the settlement south of London Bridge was notorious by the end of the sixteenth century. We can take it that the monk knew well what he was describing – his master the Bishop of Winchester was much the greatest of the area's brothel-keepers.

Since the founding of London, there must always have been a settlement across the river, and in recent years we have begun to learn how and where the Romans built around the southern end of their first bridge, and along the line of their two main roads from the coast. It seems as if they used the south bank as a centre for entertainment and spectacle, at a safe distance from their respectable homes and the official buildings.

Centuries later, south London again served the same purpose: the City was run by serious-minded money-men, who feared and detested public entertainments, and it was Southwark which became the centre for unsavoury and riotous amusements, for theatres and arenas, for brothels and the rowdiest taverns.

The most famous of the theatres to be linked with Shakespeare – the Globe – was built in 1599 with timbers taken from the Theatre in Shoreditch after a Puritan campaign had ousted playhouses from the

City. Across the river, the nearest neighbour of the new Globe was the Paris Garden, where bull-baiting, bear-baiting, dog- and cock-fights provided regular amusement.

Southwark was always home to trades which the City found objectionable, from smelly dyeworks to fish ponds, but none was so popular as debauchery in its taverns and brothels. Every new repression of vice in the City brought fresh drafts of criminals and exploiters across the river, where they were quickly visited by all the gamblers, drinkers

ELIZABETHAN
LONDON IN THE RAIN
A downpour like this would have brought raw sewerage over the thresholds of the finest houses, and washed away the floors of the hovels in which many newcomers to the capital were forced to live. It is easy to see how, on a dry day, fire could cross the narrow streets, leaping between the overhanging upper stories.

and wantons who had been their customers. The watermen who carried pleasure seekers grew rich as every class in society, from the lowest to the aristocratic, crossed the Thames for sport.

Southwark was more than just a resort for Londoners: no traveller was permitted across London Bridge at night, and to lodge late arrivals a string of inns was built close to the bridge. The guests in the taverns were far from home, with money in their pockets – as perfect a supply of victims and gullible punters as the robbers, tricksters and pimps could have wanted.

Doctor Johnson's underworld – Alsatia

> *Here malice, rapine, accident conspire,*
> *And now a rabble rages, now a fire;*
> *Their ambush here relentless ruffians lay,*
> *And here the fell attorney prowls foe prey;*
> *Here falling houses thunder on your head …*
>
> *London! the needy villain's gen'ral home …*

We know that Dr Johnson, who wrote these lines, lived to the north of Fleet Street: we may visit one of his homes, and stand in the bar of the Cheshire Cheese, where he ate and drank. Across the main street, less than thirty yards away, was a boundary Johnson could never safely cross, the edge of Alsatia. The area between Fleet Street and the muddy edge of the river had once held the Whitefriars Monastery, and when Henry VIII dissolved the monasteries he gave the buildings and land to his physician. As a religious site, this had already been a sanctuary for those fleeing justice, and at the end of the sixteenth century the local people were even successful in claiming that Whitefriars was not subject to the jurisdiction of the City. The crooks had removed themselves from the ordinary controls of the law, and the long arguments about jurisdiction gave the area its ironic nickname Alsatia – from Alsace, the area so long disputed between France and Germany.

By the time Dr Johnson was writing in the mid-eighteenth century, the law had been changed again to abolish the comfortable privileges, but it had been impossible to dislodge the criminals. By staying on the safe side of the street, Johnson might have been able to glimpse, by peering down alleys or raising his eyes to the higher windows in the houses opposite, hints of the life within. High-voiced arguments, rambling brawls, and sudden short attacks; goods and people moving in and out to signals from a street-corner lookout. Beggars mutilated and diseased, drunk and amusingly rubber-legged, drunk and angry, drunk and sentimentally despairing. Young men who thought they'd seen it all, young women who had, children with filthy, old and torn clothes, clever thieves wearing the latest and the finest. All the mad and the sad and the bad.

BEER STREET
AND GIN LANE
By 1751, when Hogarth published these pictures, London had suffered cheap gin for a generation. The artist may have flattered the cheerful prosperity of a city that drank beer, but the horrors of Gin Lane were real enough. Only the pawnbroker prospers here, taking the clothes off a carpenter, the tools of his trade and his wife's kitchen goods, to buy strong drink in a town abandoned to violence, decay and despair.

Charles Dickens' underworld – Saffron Hill

A dirtier or more wretched place he had never seen. The street was very narrow and muddy, and the air was impregnated with filthy odours. There were a good many small shops; but the only stock in trade appeared to be heaps of children who, even at that time of night, were crawling in and out at the doors, or screaming from the inside. The sole places that seemed to prosper, amid the general blight of the place, were the public-houses; and in them the lowest orders of Irish were wrangling with might and main. Covered ways and yards, which here and there diverged from the main street, disclosed little knots of houses, where drunken men and women were positively wallowing in the filth; and from several of the doorways great ill-looking fellows were cautiously emerging, bound, to all appearances, on no very well-disposed or harmless errands.

GIN LANE

VICTORIAN SLUM
STREET
*These are the slums of
Dickens's time: ancient
houses crammed into streets
in which cheap goods were
traded for meagre
livelihoods, and diseased
and ramshackle houses in
which the poor were hidden.*

This is Oliver Twist's first sight of Saffron Hill, north-west of the City, close to Sadler's Wells, as the Artful Dodger takes him to Fagin's lair.

Dickens wrote from knowledge as well as imagination; the slum he described was no more than a mile from his own home in Holborn where he wrote *Oliver Twist*. When he was young he had lived in poverty, within the Marshalsea prison where his father was held as a debtor. As a reporter, and then as a novelist, he showed comfortable Victorians just how squalid was the life of the poor whom they ignored every day, and at times his research into the low life of London became obsessive. He visited the prisons, the madhouses, witnessed executions, and made perilous voyages through the rookeries, the criminal slums of which Saffron Hill was typical.

SANCTUARY

Once there was a tower house close by Westminster Abbey, a small fort strong enough to withstand determined attack by scores of armed men. Strangely, it was built and maintained to protect criminals.

Even for an outrageous crime committed in full public view, a criminal could escape punishment if he could reach sanctuary before the hue and cry caught up with him. So long as he could reach either a church or one of the recognised precincts around a major abbey or cathedral, he was safe.

Sanctuary was a privilege established by the Saxon kings. Church properties were not to be subject to the royal writ, and no holy or consecrated place should be defiled by brawls. To escape alive was an obvious advantage for the criminal, but there was a time limit and another kind of penalty. Within forty days, he had to make a full confession of his crime to the coroner – the king's officer – and take an oath to leave the realm forever, knowing that if he did not go as agreed to his port of departure, or returned without the king's permission he could immediately be executed. There was a price for the life that was spared – the exile was now a confessed felon and all his property was forfeit to the Crown.

Every sanctified property could at first offer sanctuary, from simple parish churches to St Peter's Sanctuary at Westminster, a massive blockhouse which would withstand powerful attack. Across London, and in some provincial cities, were larger enclaves not only within church establishments, but in the surrounding streets, where entire criminal communities gathered in overpriced lodgings.

The abuse of sanctuary in these areas became scandalous – it was obvious that criminals were using their sheltered safety as a base for every kind of illegal activity. Even after the right of sanctuary was abolished in the early eighteenth century the old sanctuaries remained dens of thieves, intricate warrens into which the police would not venture. They became the rookeries of Dickens' London, and their last traces disappeared only with the vast redevelopments of the twentieth century and the night bombing raids of the London Blitz.

THE RIVER

The river is now just a grey and sluggish obstacle to the capital's traffic, carrying little more than sightseers and bulk waste, but once it was the great artery of London's life and crimes.

Until the last century the Thames was the main highway and thoroughfare of London. Before 1750 London Bridge was the only bridge downstream of Putney, and the water thronged with every variety and size of craft. Citizens of every degree found it quicker, safer and more pleasant to travel by water than along the filthy streets, and only the river could carry in the capital's food and raw materials, and carry out its manufactures.

Just as they have limousines and chauffeurs today, the wealthy commissioned luxurious barges, following the example of Sir John Norman, a fifteenth-century Lord Mayor who wanted to make a more dignified journey to the royal court at Westminster. To serve the less prosperous, there were already ferries as regular as any bus service. As early as 1372 the Corporation had set the fare from London to Westminster at twopence, and by Elizabethan times three thousand watermen plied their trade just as taxi drivers do today, picking up passengers at stairs and piers along both banks to ferry them across and along the river. As for people, so for goods: fully half of the country's shipping trade passed through London's docks, and the lightermen were the lorry-drivers and deliverymen of their time who carried goods to and from ships moored on the Thames.

So much trade was of course a powerful attraction for thieves and robbers of every kind. Dockers were always ready to pilfer when they could, hiding goods in their clothes and equipment, or dropping them over the side to be collected later by 'mudlarks' who would retrieve packages at low tide.

As the volume of traffic grew, specialist gangs developed techniques which could plunder entire cargoes: some used bribery to turn a watchman's head, some merely bullied their way on board, carrying tools and specialised items such as the 'black strip' – sacks large enough and strong enough to hold one hundred pounds of sugar, but dyed black so that they would be invisible in the mudflat darkness.

It could often be contrived simply to cut a boat loose from its moorings, then tow it or let it drift away to a safe spot where it could be stripped at leisure. Subtler thieves employed every kind of ruse to get on board – one gang would first let rats loose on a ship, then offer their services as rat-catchers; they would then be free to move throughout the boat, stealing as they went.

Many thefts were arranged with the owners of the cargoes, either to collect insurance or to assist in smuggling: the owner could then bring a cargo on which no duty had been paid right into London, and lose it to 'thieves' who would land it for him. The theft was often no more than a formality, since the watchmen and the Customs officials were easily, if expensively, bribed.

The sum of all these thefts was enormous, and along the banks of the river an entire class of fences – receivers of stolen property – established itself in warehouses and stores. They had to find space for tons and tons of tea, tobacco and sugar, coffee, rum and ginger. Both to find fresh markets and to conceal freshly stolen loads, the fences expanded their operations across the Channel, buying and chartering ships to carry the plunder to Continental ports.

For as long as London was a large and active port – until well into the 1960s – there was a large established underworld which made its living from cheating and robbing sailors, stealing cargoes and payrolls, and smuggling anything profitable. As the docks closed, thousands of hardworking stevedores and dockers lost their jobs, but there must also have been hundreds of crooks who were left abandoned, like fleas whose dog had died.

Execution Dock

The usual place for the hanging of pirates and sea-rovers, at the low-water mark, and there to remain till three tides had overflowed them.
Stow's description of Execution Dock (1598)

Public execution was always meant to overawe, to strike fear, to set tongues wagging about the fate of criminals. Just as the ceremonies at

HANGING A PIRATE
AT EXECUTION DOCK
Here on the north bank of the Thames, downstream of the City, prisoners convicted of crimes on the river and the high seas were hanged, then left on display as a warning to sailors and travellers on the river.

Tyburn and the gibbets by the highways stood as warnings to land travellers, the hangings at Execution Dock and the display of bodies along the shore were shows to impress the thousands of watermen and passengers on the river.

On land it was common to execute a prisoner close to the scene of his crime, and by the same logic river thieves and murderers, pirates and mutineers were hanged at the water's edge. On the south bank, there was a gallows on a dock where a small river joined the Thames, and the river itself took a new title. Among the many names for a hangman's noose was 'the Devil's Neckinger' (or neckcloth), and the river is still known as the Neckinger.

On the north bank in Wapping was Execution Dock, close to the old inn The Prospect of Whitby. Perhaps in the earliest times some prisoners were simply tethered to drown, but from sketches we know that the later practice was to take a portable gallows onto the foreshore close to the water, and carry out an ordinary hanging. The body would then be hanged in chains, held together by netting, at one of the river's landmarks, to remain as stark warning to passers-by until rats, birds and the elements had destroyed it.

PART 2

Crime

HIGH CRIME

History tells us few names, shows us fewer faces. Before printing and before photography, only the greatest heroes and villains found a place in the written records and the songs of the balladeers. The poor and the powerless, honest or criminal, lived and died anonymously.

The great exceptions have always been those who challenged the power of the king, the Church or the government: their crimes, and especially their punishment, had to be made known to the people. Rebellion, heresy and treason were contagions to be eliminated ruthlessly, and the culprits had to be brought to a ritual of public death, so that no whispered rumour of their survival could encourage others to rise.

Most men condemned as traitors were merely unsuccessful competitors for power, ambitious cousins of the king or nobles who misjudged the strength of their forces. Only failure made them criminal.

The stories of Lady Jane Grey, of Essex and Strafford, of Mary, Queen of Scots have been told again and again – these are the famous stories of foolish and defeated ambition. High crime here means much bolder enterprises: commoners who dared offend against the Crown and the government for gain, for their beliefs, or in raw rebellion.

THE TREASURE OF A KINGDOM

> *The Chapel of the Pyx lies within Westminster Abbey, behind a heavy studded door; it was once a royal treasury, and the pyx – a chest – held purest gold and silver, standards against which all precious metals could be tested.*
>
> *That treasury was robbed, and it is said that in his rage at the crime Edward I ordered the skin of the thief to be nailed to the chapel door.*

In 1303, in the reign of Edward I, a fisherman on the River Thames found a silver goblet in his net, and from its decoration he knew that it must have been the property of the king. More clues soon followed: behind tombstones in a churchyard in south London rich cups and dishes were found hidden; around the country large amounts of foreign money were offered to money changers; a prostitute found wearing a precious ring explained that she had received it from the sacrist of Westminster Abbey.

It seemed that royal treasure was being traded and spread across the realm while the king was hundreds of miles to the north waging war on the Scots. When word reached Edward he appointed a special commission of judges to investigate the reports. Two weeks later the truth was discovered – the king's store of jewels, plate and gold coin had been plundered.

There were two main stores of royal wealth in London, each a part of what was known as the royal Wardrobe: in the Tower of London was a store for bulky items such as arms and armour, cloth, furs and furniture; but the sort of goods which we might call treasure today, the small, the glittering and the valuable, were stored in the crypt under the chapter house of Westminster. It was this second treasury that had been raided.

John Droxford, the Keeper of the Wardrobe and the official responsible for the king's belongings, hurried back to London with the key to the crypt, and found the extent of the theft. He was quickly able to find much of the loot – some lay under the bed of the keeper of the Palace of Westminster, and still more in the lodgings of a local rogue called Richard Pudlicott. As damning evidence of betrayal, Droxford found that many of the monks had concealed stolen goods, and he ordered that every cleric – the abbot and forty-eight monks – be taken to the Tower with the other suspects. A royal commission began to hear evidence, and the chief result of their interrogation and torture was a full confession by Richard Pudlicott.

Richard was a failed clerk and wool trader who had drifted into the loose life of Westminster, where the king's servants and the monks from the Abbey led a notoriously debauched life. He had already committed one serious burglary, stealing valuable silver plate from the chapter house, but the proceeds were soon spent, and he urgently needed fresh funds. He devised a plan to rob the treasury, by tunnelling from the churchyard through thirteen feet of stone wall, and after spending most of the winter and spring in his labours, Richard was rewarded. When he broke through to the treasury he found extraordinary loot: baskets, chests, and many other vessels full of valuables, plate, relics, jewels and gold. It was a hoard worth £100,000, a year's entire revenue for the king.

These drawings from a manuscript of the time show the theft of the king's treasure, and the arrest of Pudlicott in possession of the loot. One of the soldiers is shown seizing the crown itself from the thief's head.

This appears to be the tale of a master burglar, whose careful planning and daring execution were enough to penetrate the richest vault in the kingdom. But there is another, more likely explanation which does not require us to believe that Richard abandoned drinking, gaming and every other distraction to spend months digging, nor that the citizens of Westminster saw nothing of the removal of the rubble extracted from a hole large enough to let a man make his way through a thirteen-foot wall, nor that none of the many people with business within the chapter house heard any of the hammer blows and shovelling.

Much more probable is an early, classic inside job, in which Richard's friend the sacrist provided him with a chance to force a door or break a window, a theft complete in hours rather than months. But with so many clergy among the guilty, at a time when churchmen insisted that

In this one picture the story was told of how Wat Tyler was struck down – on the left – and how the young King Richard calmed the rebels. The scene is Smithfield, and the trees may be the ancient elms long used for executions.

they were beyond the temporal laws of the king, the case created intricate and embarrassing legal and political complications. It was two years before Richard and a few very minor culprits were executed, an oddly long delay for such an outrageous crime in an age when royal fury usually meant sudden death.

It seems likely that Richard was promised clemency if he would make a confession that he worked alone, then put to death so that he could not withdraw it. If his skin was spread across the chapel door, it may well have been as a threat to his untried and unpunished accomplices among the monks, a warning that the king would tolerate no further betrayal.

THE REBELS

When Adam delved, and Eve span,
Who was then a gentleman?
The rhyme made famous by the priest John Ball
in his challenge to the rich and powerful.

In 1381 London was invaded by one hundred thousand men, an armed and angry force which put to death some of the greatest in the land, occupied the Tower of London, and destroyed great palaces by fire. This was no foreign army: the men were led from Kent by a roofer called Wat Tyler and from Essex by a priest called Jack Straw, and when they reached the capital their armies of peasants were joined by thousands of angry Londoners.

This was no mere rabble of the hungry poor: there were trained and disciplined soldiers who had fought for their king, humble priests and local gentry, prosperous small farmers. All knew that they had been exploited and cheated, and wanted justice. Taxed to pay for war in France, taxed to pay for the luxuries enjoyed by the great monasteries, obliged to labour for the lords and gentry, they finally went on the march to fight a new and corruptly extorted poll tax.

The government which had aroused the country men was also despised in the City, and the army from Kent was allowed to cross

London Bridge unopposed. Parties of men spread across the capital to open and burn down the Fleet and Marshalsea prisons, and to rampage into the Temple to destroy the homes and the records of the hated lawyers, courtiers and clergy. The main force swept to the Tower, to where the young King Richard II and the highest officers of his government had retreated.

Seizing a chance, and while the strong garrison stood aside, the mob rushed into the Tower to plunder and destroy. In the Chapel of St John they discovered three of their most hated enemies – the Archbishop of Canterbury, who was also Chancellor; Sir Robert Hales, the Lord Treasurer; and John Legge, the man who had devised the poll tax. All three, and an unfortunate physician who was found with them, were dragged from the altar out of the gates, and on to Tower Hill. There they were all roughly beheaded, their heads raised on pikes to be carried in triumphant parade through the City, and displayed on the ramparts of London Bridge.

Though they loathed his advisers, many of the rebels believed that the king would hear their pleas, sympathise with them, and give them justice. As his ministers were being killed, Richard was at Mile End, promising pardons to the rioters gathered there, and great changes which would free all peasants from their obligations to the landlords, and make them full tenants of their land. Hearing this, many of the Essex rebels were satisfied and turned for home.

Wat Tyler and the Kentish rebels agreed to meet the king at Smithfield, and the same promises of reform were offered to them, but Tyler was distrustful and demanding. When it seemed that Tyler might assault the king, he was struck down by William Walworth, Mayor of London, and soon died. With great courage Richard turned to the mob, which far outnumbered his small party, and declared himself the leader of the people. As they stood in confusion he cried 'I will be your chief and captain!' It was enough: believing that their cause had been won, the rebels dispersed and marched back to their land.

But the king's promises were hollow. When the great force had left London, Tyler's head replaced the Archbishop's on the bridge, and other leaders were pursued and seized: Jack Straw, the Essex leader, was beheaded; John Ball, a preacher whose message of freedom and justice for the poor was blamed for the unrest, was brought before the king himself to be hanged, drawn and quartered.

The Peasants' Revolt was defeated by guile and brutality, but the men of Kent were to rise again two generations later. In 1450 forty thousand followed Jack Cade to London, on an expedition that followed Tyler's path. The landowners were no longer the chief objects of hatred, but the grasping oppression of a Lord Treasurer was again notorious, and Cade found support among the merchants of the City. The Treasurer and his son-in-law the despised Sheriff of Kent were decapitated, and their heads shown to the people locked in a mocking kiss.

The casual brutality of Cade's men, the killings and the robberies, turned the City authorities against them. When they appealed to the Constable of the Tower for help, he raised a loyal force which struggled to hold London Bridge against a further assault by the rebels and was eventually able to defeat and scatter them. Cade was tracked down and wounded, to perish on his way back to the City: in just a few weeks, the rebellion which would carry his name had flared and died. Since they could not punish him in life, the authorities mutilated him in death: Cade's head was cut off, and his dismembered quarters were dragged through London as proof of his defeat.

SMITHFIELD

> *1541: – In this year was burned in Smithfield a child named Richard Mekins, this child passed not the age of 15 years, and somewhat as he had heard some other folks talk, chanced to speak against the Sacrament of the altar. This boy was accused to Edmund Bonner, Bishop of London, who so diligently followed the accusation, that he first found the means to indict him, and then arraigned him, and after burned him.*
>
> Edward Hall, *Chronicles*

Just to the north-west of the walls of London was a large smooth grassy field, a space into which Londoners spilled out from their tight streets and dark alleys, to stroll and sport, to trade and look for entertainment. Kings chose Smithfield for lavish royal tournaments, merchants held a weekly horse and livestock market, and each year the biggest and bawdiest event of the London year was held there, the vast market and carnival called Bartholomew Fair, where tens of thousands would marvel at the show and take every kind of pleasure.

Smithfield became equally famous, however, for its sinister spectacles: for four hundred years it was a place of execution. In the earliest days, it was no more than a convenient spot close to Newgate where prisoners could be led to a group of elm trees to be hanged, or to a pool for drowning. Long used for the execution of common criminals, Smithfield gained a particular notoriety as a place where political and religious enemies of the Crown were put to death.

Wat Tyler fell here, but the first of Smithfield's famous victims had been William Wallace, the Scottish resistance leader who had fought the English for thirty years before he was captured and brought to London in 1305. The execution of so notorious an enemy of the Crown had to be contrived as a public spectacle, before the greatest crowd, and for this Smithfield offered a fine arena.

BURNINGS IN
SMITHFIELD
Sending religious opponents to the stake was said to cleanse away heresy, but also gratified the deep fears and hatreds aroused in the feuds of the Reformation. This picture is taken from an edition of Foxe's Book of Martyrs, most famous of the works intended to keep alive hatred of the Catholic church – neither the words, nor the images of brave suffering, bore any relation to the squalid truth.

DEATH IN THE PILLORY

Egan and Salmon were thief-takers who lured young men into taking part in crimes, then gave false evidence against them, simply to gain the rewards paid when their victims were convicted and hanged. Though they caused many deaths, when their racket was discovered their crimes could be punished only by imprisonment and exposure in the Smithfield pillory. There an outraged screaming mob stoned them, killing Egan and maiming Salmon.

The fires of Smithfield

Tower Hill was known for the beheading of traitors, Tyburn for the hanging of criminals, but Smithfield gained particular notoriety for burnings. Death by fire may seem to us to be the cruellest of punishments, but it had a special purpose: in a time of powerful superstition, the medieval Church believed that the flames would purify and cleanse, drive out the Devil, and save the souls of witches and heretics.

Perhaps because it was perilous to build fires at the normal execution sites in the streets or market places close to the timber buildings of the City, perhaps to provide space for a larger crowd, it became common to hold burnings on open land. There was at first no set pattern – Tower Hill seems to have been used before Smithfield, and courts and kings occasionally prescribed unpleasantly ingenious methods such as roasting the prisoner within a cage.

Boiling

In 1520 a new and terrible punishment was inflicted for the first time at Smithfield. A man called Richard Rose was believed to have poisoned a quantity of yeast in an attempt to murder his master the Bishop of Lancaster. Though the bishop himself survived, seventeen others died, and a new sentence was laid down for anyone convicted of murdering a master or a spouse: they must be boiled alive.

Poor Rose was probably innocent – such outbreaks of food poisoning are now better understood – but he was placed in a huge cauldron slung over a pile of logs, and died two hours after the fire was lit. Later poisoners were shown a little mercy, and thrown into water or oil only after it had been brought to the boil.

Martyrs

It was the religious persecutions of Tudor times which gave the fires of Smithfield their lasting notoriety. After Henry VIII had dramatically seized control of the English Church, he and his successors fought political and religious vendettas in which both Protestants and Catholics went to the stake.

Smithfield became associated in particular with Protestant martyrdoms. Forty-three of the Protestants put to death during the

47

reign of Queen Mary were burned there, seven in a single day. In the nineteenth century a large quantity of their charred remains was unearthed during building work, together with what appeared to be a stake with its iron neck collar still attached.

The memory of the Smithfield burnings has been kept alive by religious extremists, who still publish the fanciful and downright dishonest accounts given by Foxe in his *Book of Martyrs*. Though often despised as Bloody Mary, we can now see that Mary Tudor was probably the most merciful of her dynasty. After this period, Tyburn became the main place of execution, and as London grew, Smithfield went into a long decline, becoming the unsavoury haunt of ruffians and duellists, until the area was drained, paved and fenced at the beginning of the seventeenth century. In 1638 it became the centre of London's meat trade, with a market and slaughterhouses; though the great fair continued to be held for another two centuries, it became notoriously squalid, and was abolished in 1855.

THE DEATH FOR TRAITORS

> 'You ... must be removed to the prison from which you came, and on ..., your body to be drawn on a sledge to the place of execution; there to be hanged but not until you are dead; your bowels to be taken out, your body quartered, your head cut off and affixed at the King's disposal; and the Lord have mercy on your soul.'

The most terrible of all lawful punishments was the elaborate execution prescribed for traitors. Although courts might from time to time employ some novel and appalling sentence – boiling alive, or drowning – to fit a particular crime, it was laid down for seven hundred years that the enemies of the Crown should be hanged, drawn and quartered.

Each element in this state ritual served a purpose, not only to inflict physical pain but to demonstrate the traitor's defeat and expose him to public humiliation and pain. The prisoner was first dragged through the streets behind a horse. When some early prisoners were so broken by the journey that they arrived at the scaffold dead or insensible, it was

DOCTOR CAMERON ON THE ROAD TO TYBURN

Archibald Cameron was the last man to be executed for treason after the Jacobite Rebellion of 1745. His crime was to have joined the rebels, not as a soldier but as a physician to the Young Pretender; he fled abroad but was captured on his return. The picture shows the first part of the sentence for treason – he was dragged on a sledge from the Tower to Tyburn. By the standards of the time, some mercy was shown in carrying out the rest of his sentence; Cameron was allowed to hang until dead before being decapitated.

ordered that they be towed on a hurdle or sledge. This was no humane order – for maximum effect the prisoner had to be alive and conscious during the torments to follow.

The next stage was a conventional hanging, but contrived so that the prisoner should not be killed; if the knot of the hangman's rope was placed directly behind his head, or under his chin, he would be strangled slowly, and the executioner could cut him down after some minutes and revive him.

Once lifted down, the prisoner was laid out nearby, and slow butchery began. Some prisoners were castrated, all were slit open so that their intestines could be brought out to be burned before their eyes. This was the drawing, the pulling out of internal organs, the hangman cutting and tugging much as a cook might gut a fish or a fowl before cooking. Some prisoners' hearts were cut out to be displayed to the crowd. The prisoner was then beheaded, and the head held high with the traditional cry of 'Behold the head of a traitor!' Then his body would be quartered with axe and knife, and every part of the man was then plunged into a ready heated cauldron, for parboiling in water heavily laced with salt and herbs to preserve it and deter carrion birds. When this was done, a coating of hot pitch or tar was applied to seal each section against the weather.

Thus prepared, the pieces of the traitor were then carried away to be put on show. Along the walls of the Tower bodies were hung, and heads raised on pikes, food for the ravens until the bones were picked clean. Much the most famous exhibition in London was high on the gatehouse at the southern end of London Bridge. The first head to be displayed there was that of the Scottish patriot William Wallace, executed in 1305; to relay the grim message of his defeat to sympathisers in the North, his quarters were carried to Newcastle, Berwick, Perth and Stirling.

Dividing the body was barbaric, but with a clear purpose. The greatest fear was that treason would beget treason, that the followers of a rebel would rise again to overthrow the Crown. It was a common belief that a man's body had to be whole for him to enter the afterlife (this is why the anatomists were so feared) and in cutting up the traitor's body the authorities were destroying not only a mortal body, but an immortal soul.

After Wallace came many more: Cardinal Fisher's head was removed because it seemed not to decay, but to look healthier with each passing day '... so that in his lifetime he never looked so well', and the authorities were alarmed when this preservation was seen as a miracle by the credulous. Although his body had been given a dignified burial within the chapel of the Tower, Sir Thomas More's head stood on London Bridge until his daughter was able to persuade the bridge

EXECUTION ON KENNINGTON COMMON
South of the Thames, Kennington was a rival to Tyburn. In the same carnival spirit, executions in Surrey were carried out on Kennington Common, and when both sites were to be used on the same day Londoners had to choose which spectacle to attend. These Scots rebels died traitors' deaths surrounded by a vast crowd.

watchman to release it to her; she kept the boxed head with her until she died, when it joined her in a Canterbury church vault.

London Bridge was used for display because all land travellers from the south would have to pass beneath the heads and take heed of the dreadful warning against treason. Other City gates were used in just the same way – one writer noted that when new heads were spiked on Temple Bar, over the Strand, enterprising men were charging passers-by a halfpenny each to take a closer look through a telescope.

The greatest revolt against the Crown was of course the Civil War and the execution of Charles I. After the Restoration, the men who had signed Charles' death warrant were butchered at Charing Cross, close to where the king had died. On 20 October 1660 the diarist Pepys wrote 'This afternoon … I saw the limbs of some of our new traytors set upon Aldersgate, which was a sad sight to see; and a bloody week this and the last have been, there being ten hanged, drawn and quartered.'

A strange posthumous revenge was taken against Cromwell, who had already died. The Lord Protector had been buried in Westminster Abbey, but his body was dug up and dragged to Tyburn, to be ceremonially hanged for a day with those of two other regicides, then buried beneath the gallows. The heads were cut off and taken to Westminster Hall where Charles had been tried, to be impaled on long poles high on the roof. They remained there for more than forty years until a great storm blew down the empty skulls.

Hanging, drawing and quartering was not abolished as the punishment for treason until 1870, though nearly a century had then passed since the full ritual had been employed: from the seventeenth century it had become common to leave the prisoner hanging until he was quite dead.

THE GUNPOWDER PLOT

Remember, remember
The Fifth of November:
Gunpowder, Treason and Plot.
I see no reason
Why gunpowder treason
Should ever be forgot.

In other lands the people light fires and fill the skies with fireworks to celebrate days of liberation or independence, the birthdays of heroes and heroines. In Britain, each November, children make effigies of a notorious and unsuccessful traitor, parade them in the streets to beg, with a shout of 'Penny for the Guy', and then on the fifth day set them proudly on bonfires, to watch as they are eaten by the flames. Every year we re-enact the cruel public destruction of a great traitor.

Guy Fawkes, every child has been told, tried to blow up the Houses of Parliament as King James I was opening the new session on 5 November 1605. The lives of more than five hundred people were saved only by a chance tip-off. The resulting midnight search by lantern-light revealed a vast store of gunpowder barrels in the crypt under the Palace of Westminster and the cornered Fawkes, crouching ready to light the fuse. Fawkes turned out to be just one of a gang of ruthless conspirators, fanatical Catholics who did not flinch from mass murder to overthrow the Protestant king and his legitimate government.

Fawkes' capture was dramatic enough in itself to be memorable, yet we celebrate the plot because it has served so many political purposes to keep the story alive – Royalists see the threat to the king, Parliamentarians the attempt to kill so many public representatives, Protestants find in the plot vivid proof of the danger from Papist plotters. For their part, Catholics have found inspiration in the bravery of Fawkes as he resisted 'uttermost torture' for three days to allow his confederates time to flee, and evidence of their oppression in the public cruelty of the plotters' execution.

But how much of the famous story is true? Fawkes was a tall, red-bearded soldier of fortune, a religious convert who had made his way to

THE GUNPOWDER PLOTTERS

The execution of the Gunpowder plotters was public, prolonged and foul: a display of royal vengeance intended not only to punish but to intimidate all opposition. They were drawn to execution on hurdles, hanged and quartered, and their heads displayed.

Flanders to join the Catholic Englishmen fighting for the Spanish against the Protestant Dutch, and then went to Spain to urge Philip III to invade England and depose James I. When he returned to Flanders he was recruited by a man called Winter to return to England and join a secret group plotting against the king. Fawkes, Winter, and their confederates Catesby, Wright and Percy swore an oath of secrecy and began their preparations.

Their first move was to rent a house next to the Palace of Westminster, and in December 1604 they began work on a tunnel which would extend right under Parliament itself. The work went well at first, but an even better opportunity came when, early the following year, they were able to take over from a coal-merchant the lease on a ground-floor cellar below the House of Lords. Thirty-six barrels of gunpowder were carried across the river in great secrecy, to be hidden under stacks of firewood.

The aim was always to kill the king and Parliament together, but for such a devastating blow the plotters wanted permission to proceed from Sir William Stanley, leader of the English Catholics in exile. In the spring and early summer of 1605 Fawkes tried to confer with Stanley, but by the time he had secured agreement and returned to England, an outbreak of the plague had forced Parliament into recess, and it was not to meet again until 5 November.

On the night of the 4th, all preparations were complete, and Fawkes sat ready to light the fuse. But the thought of killing five hundred men, many of whom were decent and sympathetic, seems to have pricked the conscience of someone concerned in the plot, because more than a week before, on 26 October, an anonymous letter had been delivered to Lord Monteagle. It warned him to stay away from the opening of Parliament, which was to receive 'a terrible blow'.

We now suspect that government agents had long known of the plot. Perhaps the letter was written and delivered by a spy, perhaps it was merely a contrivance agreed with Monteagle. According to the conventional story, Monteagle was quick to inform the authorities, but the king himself was not told of the threat until the 4th. This delay may have been intended to make sure that no leak betrayed to the plotters that they had been discovered, perhaps it was a clever stage management of events to make a last-minute discovery seem more startling and dramatic. When the king was informed, he ordered an immediate search by Sir Thomas Knyvet, a Westminster magistrate, and it was his men who discovered Fawkes and his lethal store.

Fawkes was dragged before the king, and defiantly declared that 'a desperate deed requires a desperate remedy'. James ordered that Fawkes should be taken to the Tower and subjected to terrible increasing torture until he betrayed all his accomplices. Fawkes proved his courage by withstanding torture for three days as his fellow conspirators fled north. Catesby, Percy and Winter were tracked down in Staffordshire, only Winter surviving a bitter fight; seven others implicated in the plot were tried with Fawkes at Westminster Hall. All were inevitably sentenced to be hanged, drawn and quartered, the prescribed penalty for treason.

On 30 January 1606, five of the plotters were executed in St Paul's

Churchyard, Fawkes and the two others in Old Palace Yard, Westminster. Fawkes still feeble from the destruction of his body by torture, was barely able to climb the ladder of the gallows.

THE KILLING OF A KING

The Civil War had been fought and lost. The armies of King Charles I had lost the Battle of Naseby nearly three years before, and after Cromwell had defeated an army raised in Scotland to replace Charles on the throne, Charles was captured.

Now in January 1649 Charles sat in the Great Hall of the Palace of Westminster, charged with treason for making war 'against the parliament and kingdom of England', an indictment and a trial contrived by Cromwell to give legal form to the killing of a king.

Through all four days of his trial Charles sat defiantly wearing his hat, refusing to enter a plea or acknowledge in any way the authority of the court. This was in part a show of the arrogance and certainty of his own divine right of kingship which had weakened his reign, but he must also have known that there could be no outcome but his own death – to protest or defend himself could only cost him his dignity.

At ten o'clock on the morning of 30 January, two days after the trial, Charles was taken from St James' Palace to walk through the park between two lines of soldiers to his palace in Whitehall. A vast crowd had already gathered to fill the street, held back by a cordon of troops; at every window, on every roof, spectators waited quietly.

This was no drunken Tyburn mob; though Londoners had supported Parliament against the king, the mood was solemn. Charles had prepared himself for his last appearance before his people, instructing his hairdresser carefully, and dressing in three shirts in case onlookers should mistake a shiver in the cold air for a betrayal of cowardice.

Outside the Banqueting Hall of Whitehall a broad scaffold had been erected, its platform level with the first floor, and waiting upon it were the low block, the axe, and an executioner who was wearing not only his mask but a wig and false beard, for fear of being recognised. Charles stepped out into the open air through a tall window: he had prepared a speech, and although the crowds were being held too far back to hear his words, he addressed the group on the scaffold.

Then he carefully removed his cloak and doublet, said his one last word 'Remember' to the Bishop of London, and lowered his neck to the block. When the axe fell, 'There was such a dismal universal groan amongst the thousands of people … as I never heard before and desire I may not hear again.'

Charles' body and head were placed in the vault at Windsor which

THE EXECUTION OF KING CHARLES I
This recollection of the killing of the king may not be accurate in every detail, but captures the crowd in a sombre, even a horrified mood. Years later, when the men who had ordered Charles's death were condemned, they were taken to the foot of Whitehall to face the spot where the King had died as they were beheaded.

held Henry VIII, but in 1813 the royal surgeon, Sir Henry Halford rediscovered the body and performed an autopsy. Sir Henry secretly made off with Charles' fourth cervical vertebra, the bone from his neck which had been severed by the axe, and for thirty years took delight in shocking his dinner guests by displaying it as a salt cellar. Queen Victoria was not at all amused when she heard about this, and ordered that the bone be returned to the coffin.

THE CRIME OF COLONEL BLOOD

No treasure was more precious than the Crown Jewels, no stronghold mightier than the Tower of London. How could anyone steal such a prize?

In 1671, as now, the Tower of London was open to visitors, who came to marvel at the castle itself with its sinister history, to see the lions and bears in the royal menagerie, and to marvel at the Crown Jewels. In those days the Martin Tower, at the north-east corner far from the gates, was used as the Jewel House, and it provided a home and a livelihood to an elderly custodian called Talbot Edwards. It was a simple arrangement – when visitors asked permission to see the Jewels, Edwards took a small fee, showed them into the strongroom and opened the heavy doors of a great cupboard to reveal the display.

Edwards and his wife seem to have been kindly folk. It was Mrs Edwards who looked after the wife of a visiting country parson when she turned faint, and when the couple returned a few days later it was to bring a present as a token of their gratitude. Friendship quickly grew, and they even discussed a little matchmaking: the clergyman had a nephew looking for a wife, perhaps the pretty Edwards girl would catch his eye? It was agreed that the families should meet more formally, at the Martin Tower, on 9 May.

The parson was in fact Colonel Thomas Blood, a schemer and adventurer who had gained his rank fighting in the Parliamentary army during the Civil War. As a reward for service he also took for himself valuable estates confiscated from Royalists, but he lost three when the

*Here is Blood's gang as it
took flight, the strongroom
open on the right, Edwards
beaten and stabbed on the
ground, the robbers
wrapping their loot as they
run – it seems that Blood
himself is the central thief,
hugging the orb.*

monarchy was restored in 1660, and Blood joined in a number of plots against the Crown. When each plot failed in turn and his co-conspirators fell into Royalist hands, Blood always made good his escape, and the suspicion grew that he had kept his freedom by betraying his fellows.

When Blood arrived at the Tower on the 9th, in his clerical disguise, he was rather early, but explained that his nephew would soon follow. He had with him two friends: to pass the time, could they be shown the

Jewels? Edwards was happy to agree, but no sooner had he opened the strongroom than he was grabbed, and a cloak thrown over his head. When he struggled, he was clubbed, and finally Blood stabbed him in the stomach with his sword.

As Edwards lay dreadfully wounded, the robbers made ready to smuggle out their loot: Blood crushed the Crown and hid it beneath his cloak, one accomplice took the Orb, and the third man set about cutting the Sceptre in half. Just then they were interrupted by Edwards' son, the robbery was discovered, and with a cry of 'Treason! The Crown is stolen!' Edwards' daughter raised the hue and cry. A crowd chased Blood and his men out across the drawbridge, wild shots were fired, and in a struggle precious stones from the regalia were scattered about. The

COLONEL BLOOD
This is the face of the adventurer, the patient and cunning plotter who brutally seized the Crown Jewels, yet a man subtle and persuasive enough to avoid all punishment.

thief with the Orb had tucked it down his breeches and found he could not run, so he tossed it into the crowd and escaped in the confusion. Blood still had the Crown, reached his horse and would have made his escape had his mount not slipped and fallen. When arrested, Blood seems to have been astoundingly cool. 'It was a bold attempt,' he observed, 'but it was for a Crown.' He then calmly and persistently refused to be questioned by anyone but the king himself, and to the surprise of many the king agreed.

It seemed there could be only one fate for an old enemy of the king caught in a violent act of treason. Guy Fawkes had been tortured and cruelly executed for an attempt on the life of his grandfather, his father had been beheaded by the Colonel's Parliamentarian friends, yet Charles not only allowed Blood to go free, he even gave him back the disputed estates. We shall never know why. Colonel Blood was a clever rogue, and may have spun an extraordinary tale for the king, but it is hard to imagine how he explained away so obvious a treason. Some people, remembering the suspicion about Blood's true loyalties, have suggested that he was acting as the king's agent all along – had he not said it was 'for a Crown'? – and that he was pardoned and bribed to keep the scheme a secret. But then, it would have been much easier for Charles to make certain of Blood's silence by ordering a secret trial and a speedy execution.

THE ASSASSINATION OF A PRIME MINISTER

Four Presidents of the United States, an Archduke of the Austro-Hungarian Empire, a Bolshevik leader in Mexican exile ... and an unremembered Englishman.

Though there have been attempts to murder monarchs and Prime Ministers, there has been just one assassination of a head of government in Britain. On the afternoon of 11 May 1812, a tall man lay in wait behind a door within the Lobby of the Houses of Parliament.

THE SHOOTING OF
SPENCER PERCEVAL
*This was the scene when tall,
deranged John Bellingham
tried to satisfy an obscure
private grievance by shooting
the Prime Minster in the
lobby of the House of
Commons.*

As his target approached, he drew a pistol, fired once, and with a final cry of 'Murder!' the Prime Minister fell dying. The assassin did not flee, and when he was seized said simply 'My name is Bellingham; it is a private injury – I know what I have done – it was a denial of justice on the part of the Government.'

Alarmed that this was the first move of a larger uprising, the Cabinet took immediate steps to secure the capital, including the drastic stopping of all mail. Under strong military escort, Bellingham was removed to Newgate, and under questioning it emerged that he was a man with an ancient grievance about the failure of a business venture in Russia, for which he blamed the English ambassador. He had petitioned the Prince Regent and the Prime Minister, but when he still had no satisfaction, he had bought pistols and planned his revenge.

For all that Bellingham was plainly a man on the brink of insanity, the government rushed him to trial and execution – just one week later, with troops stationed to control the City and all reserves mobilised to quell any mob, Bellingham went to the gallows. Both the victim and the murderer were unremarkable men, and soon forgotten. It remains an irony that for all the plots, all the fears of violence, Perceval is the only Prime Minister to have been assassinated.

THE CATO STREET CONSPIRACY

> *Napoleon had been defeated at Waterloo five years before, but the memory of revolution in France still frightened the English ruling class. Peace brought hardship and political unrest at home – something had to be done.*

At the beginning of the nineteenth century, England was still ruled by the Old Corruption – political power was still in the hands of landowners who used Parliament and public office to run the country for their own benefit. But the world had changed, and the future was to lie with manufacture and trade, wealth created in the industrial Midlands and North. Workers were on the move from country to town, fleeing an old exploitation only to find that urban life was no kinder.

Landowners and the metropolitan rich still ruled, but the successful revolt of the American colonies and the dramatic events of the French Revolution seemed to show that a people could rise against oppression, and new ideas of the worth of the common man, of liberty and justice, were broadcast in pamphlets and declaimed from public platforms.

Though few of the campaigners favoured violence, the ruling classes were deeply frightened. To them, any pressure for change must be treason, inspired by foreigners or traitors; public demonstrations must be suppressed, any group of agitators infiltrated, rooted out, brought to book. They failed to see that this was the beginning of politics for the common people. Ordinary men and women were no longer just The Mob, angry but with power only to destroy, but people whose new literacy was bringing them knowledge and understanding.

The most shocking confrontation came in 1819. A large and peaceful crowd gathered on St Peter's Fields in Manchester to hear a radical speaker, but in panic the magistrates ordered the yeomanry – a mounted militia drawn from the gentry and the owning class – to disperse them. What followed was an undisciplined, savage attack; the militiamen were overtaken by class hatred and charged with sabres drawn, to kill at least eleven and leave many hundreds broken and wounded. In wry contempt for this use of military force, the attack was soon dubbed the Peterloo Massacre.

Expecting massive popular outrage after Peterloo, the government tightened laws and made plans to contain a revolution. It never came, but in despair and frustration a small group resolved to take action, a gesture which they hoped would stir the people to action. This was the Cato Street Conspiracy.

The leader of the group was Arthur Thistlewood, an impoverished ex-officer who felt a powerful personal calling to save the country from its oppressors, but who had recently been accused of spying for the government. If he could perform one extraordinary deed, he could prove his allegiance to the cause, and he took few precautions as he cast about for men who would join him in a desperate venture.

Meeting secretly in a stable loft in Cato Street the conspirators considered how the first blow might be struck. George Edwards, an artist, suggested blowing up the House of Commons, to succeed where Guy Fawkes had failed. When Thistlewood rejected this as punishing the innocent with the guilty, Edwards proposed an attack on ministers at a reception given by the Spanish ambassador – but Thistlewood opposed this too. There would be ladies present, and he 'shuddered with horror at the idea of that', remembering the attack on women at Peterloo.

Eventually Edwards made a proposal which won the votes of the entire group: they would launch an attack on the government at a Cabinet dinner. All the hated ministers, including the Duke of Wellington, would be put to death. The heads of the most despised would be hacked off for public display on pikes; a 'Provisional Government' would be proclaimed on posters throughout the city; the Tower of London and the Mansion House would be fired, the Bank of England plundered. Inspired by such public success the people must rise at last.

Alerted by a newspaper notice that the government was to dine in Grosvenor Square, twenty of the plotters laid in weapons and explosives, and gathered one last time in Cato Street on the night of 23 February 1820, ready for action. Suddenly, to a shout of 'We are officers! Seize their arms!' a party of Bow Street Runners burst in. In a short fight, Thistlewood ran his sword through one of the officers, who fell back dead. During the raid nine men were arrested, the others breaking out through a cordon of soldiers; Thistlewood was among the escapers, but he was arrested next day.

As traitors, the conspirators were taken to the Tower of London to be confined separately: Thistlewood was held in the Bloody Tower. At their trial every detail of the plot was set out – here was proof that the nation was in peril from desperate men, and vindication of the government's stern measures. The verdicts were inevitable, and while five of the captured men were sentenced to transportation, Thistlewood and the remaining four were condemned to death.

The executions took place outside Newgate, and as a final theatrical indignity it was ordered that the Cato Street plotters should be beheaded, the traditional punishment for traitors. There would be no headsman with an axe, however: the men were hanged together, and the bodies laid out. An unknown masked man, who appeared to have the skills of a surgeon, used a knife to decapitate each corpse in turn, and held up the head to the crowd with the old cry of 'Here is the head of a traitor!' These were the very last beheadings in Britain.

THE ARREST OF
THE CATO STREET
CONSPIRATORS
The plotters gathered to arm themselves before setting out to slaughter the Cabinet, but their naïve plans had long been betrayed. A force of Bow Street Runners raided the loft in which they were hiding, a vicious fight broke out, and those few who escaped were swiftly hunted down.

Edwards, the man who had persuaded the conspirators to attack the Cabinet, did not go to the scaffold. Nor was he transported. He was in fact a government agent, a *provocateur*, who had from the beginning informed the authorities of all the plans: the report of the dinner in Grosvenor Square was false, planted to bring the plotters together so that they could be seized. The genuine conspirators had certainly intended great harm but they were cleverly manipulated, and the puppetmasters were helped not only to push through new laws, but to carry the next election.

Low Crime

Common criminals live and die unremembered. There is always a new villain, a new outrage for the gossips to report and the writers to record: even public death brought no lasting fame when so many went to the gallows every year.

The Footpads

There was nowhere within the City of London quite so dangerous as the roads leading into it. Around the capital, beyond the reach of the Sheriffs, and where no hue and cry could be raised, robbers waited to plunder and to kill.

Between the medieval towns and cities of England great forests still grew, where early robbers lived as outlaws, though less romantically than the Robin Hood of legend and cinema. Outlawry was total exclusion from society, and any outlaw could be killed on sight; honest occupations were closed to him, and a crude survival by poaching and theft was all that remained. Robbers formed bands to protect themselves and to plunder, the bands in turn formed alliances, divided their territory, and gave an illicit sanctuary to every kind of outcast: criminals, exiles who had returned, runaway serfs and discharged soldiers.

Sometimes these robber forces reached the size of small armies: in 1248 two foreign merchants with a substantial escort were attacked at Alton, on the London–Southampton road, by six hundred men (of whom three hundred were later hanged). Intriguingly, this was one of the robberies in which local worthies took part; it seems that when the prize was a rich one, highway robbery was as tempting as smuggling and wrecking were to become along the coasts, and attracted respectable citizens. Members of royal households, even a group of monks, turned to robbery.

It may seem odd that so crude and brutal a crime should be so acceptable, but this was an age in which local loyalties ranked higher than any national patriotism, and highway victims – not only foreigners, but British travellers from other regions – were strangers passing through. Among the most common victims were the royal tax collectors: it must have gratified many men to pay their taxes, then snatch back the money the next day in a quiet spot some miles down the road.

Though those Alton robbers were hunted down, it was much more common for the authorities to take no action; they had no forces to patrol the highways and no detectives to investigate crime. It was much easier to wait for a betrayal to place a thief in their hands, then hang him as an example. A practical alternative to hanging, since the leader of an important gang would control large parts of his county, was to put him to work hunting rival gangs. Some of the most notorious highway robbers were pardoned and taken into the king's service in this way.

Then came powerful kings who imposed their will on the medieval chaos of religious and political rivalries, who won the struggle for power between Church and State, steadily subordinated even the strongest nobles, and colonised Wales, Scotland and Ireland. Strong central rule, with its national systems of law, left no room for freelance brigandry. There were to be no more merrie men, only common thieves.

Highway robbery came to take two forms, viewed quite differently by the people, if not by the law. There was a sharp division by class: those who robbed on foot were the poor and desperate, feared and loathed as base criminals, but the highwayman on horseback became a romantic figure.

The highwaymen will have a chapter (see page 70) of their own, but what of the footpads? Many were townsmen who made their way to the edges of town to make their criminal living, a much less risky undertaking than stealing in the streets. It was a trade which depended on information for consistent success, and started from inside knowledge or sharp observation. At its simplest, this meant no more than spotting the fat purse of a man on his way out of town, but thieves also used an army of informants who would point out a big spender for a share in any loot. Too often an unguarded word in a City tavern, or an attempt to impress a bawd in one of the Bankside brothels would tell thieves all they needed to set up an ambush.

In those days, routes such as Knightsbridge and Tottenham Court Road were open highways bordered by ditches and fields, notorious for the robbers who lay in wait along them. To steal from those journeying to London, City thieves would make their way to the inns just one day's travel from the capital, to look over the travellers. Innkeepers were notoriously ready to help them, even introducing thieves as honest trustworthy men who would protect a worried stranger.

Such a prepared robbery, where thief and victim had already met, could be especially dangerous for the traveller. Knowing that they would inevitably hang if captured, footpads were ruthless, ready to kill rather than risk just one survivor raising the alarm or identifying them at a trial – a body dumped or buried in the woods was unlikely to be found. If they seemed to be losing the skirmish, guards often abandoned their loads and their masters to flee.

Most footpads worked in loose alliances, two or three at a time, and always wary of betrayal, but occasionally gangs were assembled which became powerful and skilled. In the 1720s the splendidly named Obadiah Lemon led one of the bands which specialised in the robbing of coaches. A carriage was a 'rattler', and stealing from them was known as 'the rattling lay'. Lemon's first innovation was to adapt a fishing technique once used to steal through house windows. With a hook and line his men could snatch hats, wigs, and scarves from passing carriages; it was then easy to escape while the coach came to a confused halt, and no driver could pursue men dodging away on foot.

Carriage builders found a solution: they fitted perforated tin shutters to the windows, which gave excellent protection against fish-hooks but left passengers in hot dark discomfort. Meanwhile Lemon's men grew bolder – they lay in wait where a coach would have to slow for a bridge or a ford, then leaped onto the back, and climbed to slash through the roof and grab what they could. The rewards were still small, and the gang had to find a way to seize the greatest prize – the strongbox carried under the driver's seat.

Their first, stealthy method was to have one member of the gang slash at the leather straps on which the body of the coach was slung. Once these were cut, the coach was disabled, and as the driver climbed down to look over the damage, the thieves would launch themselves from cover to snatch the precious box. As the gang grew larger, greedier and more determined, it turned to cruder methods, blocking the coach's path with any convenient branches, then firing a couple of pistol shots through its windows as warning to any guard or bold passenger. This gang was ultimately destroyed by Jonathan Wild, with the well-rewarded help of Lemon himself. He fell in with Wild, became one of his closest assistants and made many appearances in court, not as a defendant but as a witness who found profit in testifying against his accomplices.

Highway robbery was interrupted, but not ended, by the creation of the Bow Street Horse Patrol, which kept watch on the approaches to the capital. Many of the robbers went into exile in the provinces, to return when the pennypinching authorities refused to fund the Patrol. The last great revival came around 1820 when there were still thousands of horse-drawn coaches making slow progress on roads so neglected that they were in worse condition than when the Romans left. Within a decade the Metropolitan Police had been founded, but a still greater threat to the livelihood of the robbers came on 15 September 1830: the world's first passenger train service opened between Liverpool and Manchester. The highwaymen and footpads were to be robbed of their prey.

THE HIGHWAYMEN

Whatever might be the way in which a journey was performed, the travellers, unless they were numerous and well armed, ran considerable risk of being stopped and plundered. The mounted highwayman ... was to be found on every main road.

Macaulay, in his *History of England*, describing the state of the land in 1685.

Highway robbery was a fitting crime for a gentleman: to be a highwayman demanded dash and elan, the spirit of a light cavalryman, with none of the skulking, nor the manual labour, of the burglar, none of the underhand wiles of the pickpocket. It was a profession which was not open to the lowest, since it first required capital to provide the swift horse and the brace of pistols, nor to the base coward who lacked the courage to stand alone, risking all on quick wits and a fast horse.

The most sordid crimes often look nobler with hindsight, but this fine romantic view of the highwaymen began while they were still at work: even when infuriated by highway robberies, Londoners made romantic heroes of the thieves themselves, enjoyed telling tales of their daring, and cheered them all along the road to the gallows.

The simplest way to explain this contradiction is to see the highwayman not as a criminal but as an outlaw, an heir to the Robin Hood of legend, who could ambush the wicked Sheriff of Nottingham then melt away into the forest. Robin Hood was supposed to have been a noble robbed of his inheritance, and the public still enjoyed hearing about high-born gentlemen who robbed only the rich.

No one fitted the popular ideal better than Sir John Popham. When he was a law student at Oxford University, and had married very respectably at the age of twenty, Popham was seized by the spirit of adventure and took to highway robbery. This was no passing whim – he spent the next ten years robbing and living the life of a criminal, until his wife persuaded him to return to the law.

Once he had abandoned crime, Popham was astonishingly successful. He was called to the Bar at the Middle Temple, elected to Parliament,

AMBUSH ON
HOUNSLOW HEATH
*Highwaymen and their
traditional prey. The
carriages of the gentry
yielded fine plunder in an
age when wealth was carried
in gold and jewels, but this
victim is prepared – he has a
blunderbuss ready to see off
the robbers.*

and at forty became a Privy Councillor. His criminal past was well known, but did not prevent his promotion to Solicitor General, Attorney General, and finally Lord Chief Justice – it was Popham who presided at the trials of Essex, Sir Walter Raleigh and Guy Fawkes. Despite his underworld experience he was a severe judge and showed little sympathy to defendants – during one trial he recognised the prisoner and asked what had happened to their old companions. The rueful reply was: 'All the villains are hanged, my lord, except you and me.'

The very Elizabethan virtues of quick wits and a way with words were also supposed to be characteristic of highwaymen. When the dramatist Ben Jonson was held up by a highwayman he tried to disconcert him by answering in verse:

> *Fly, villain, hence, or by thy coat of steel*
> *I'll make thy heart my leaden bullet feel,*
> *and send that thricely thievish soul of thine*
> *To Hell, to wean the Devil's valentine.*

But Jonson had met his match; the robber was Walter Tracey, a young man of good family who had been sent down from Oxford University, and he replied:

> *Art thou great Ben? or the revived ghost*
> *Of famous Shakespeare? or some drunken host*
> *Who, being tipsy with thy muddy beer,*
> *Dost think thy rhymes will daunt my soul with fear?*
> *Nay, know, base slave, that I am one of those*
> *Can take a purse as well in verse, as prose;*
> *And when thou art dead, write this upon thy hearse,*
> *'Here lies a poet who was robbed in verse.'*

Every good legend deserves a little embellishment, and the story went that later that same day Jonson was attacked by footpads who stole his horse, then left him and his companions tied up in a field. One of the party cried out that they were undone, but another tartly replied 'Pray, if you are all of you undone, come and undo me.'

Jonson gave literary immortality to another highwayman: in *The Alchemist* he describes a face 'cast worse than Gamaliel Ratsey' – this was a reference to the hideous mask worn by a robber of that name. Ratsey, another well-born highwayman, was said to have forced victims who had no money to entertain him by performing elaborate forfeits, according to their talents. Thus an actor had to recite a scene from Hamlet at gunpoint, and a Cambridge scholar had to deliver a learned oration. A favourite story was that when Ratsey demanded a free roadside shave from a barber who claimed to be penniless, he found twenty guineas hidden in a pot which the nervous victim dropped at his feet.

Since the highwayman depended on surprise and a swift getaway for his success, he could often avoid violence; in harsh times, this helped to elevate the profession above mere ruffianism. John Clavel, one of the very few captured highwaymen to avoid the gallows, was just the type of

GIBBETS ON HOUNSLOW HEATH
Where Heathrow Airport now spreads was once open land notorious for the ambushes of highwaymen and footpads. If they were captured, and hanged at Tyburn, their bodies were taken back to be strung up in irons, or displayed in high cages, along the roads leading into London from the West.

gentlemanly amateur that the public admired. In a brief but notorious career he specialised in holding up mail coaches on Gad's Hill and Shooter's Hill, but he pleaded at his trial 'he had never struck or wounded any man, had never taken anything from their bodies, as rings, etc., never cut their girths or saddles, or done them, when he robbed, any corporeal violence.'

Sentenced to death, Clavel wrote a verse petition to the king:

> I that have robbed so oft am now bid stand,
> Death and the Law assault me, and demand
> My life and means. I never used men so,
> But having taken their money let them go.
> Yet must I die? And is there no relief?
> The King of Kings had mercy on a thief.
> So may our gracious King too, if he please,
> Without his council, grant me a release.
> God is his precedent, and men shall see
> His mercy go beyond severity.

It worked. Clavel's life was spared, and he went on to write a longer work called *Recantation of an Ill-led Life* which went even further, and earned him a full pardon.

Most highwaymen must have been low-born and illiterate, but the reputation of the profession was so strong that criminals who took to the road would put on fine clothes and a chivalrous manner. One German visitor wrote that 'They assure you they are very sorry that poverty has driven them to that shameful recourse, and end by demanding your purse in the most courteous manner.'

After the Civil War, new recruits took to the road. When the Parliamentary forces had defeated and executed King Charles, many Royalists became fugitives: restless soldiers who could not return to their old lives, they chose to live beyond the law:

> Nor beg nor cheat will I – I scorn the same;
> but while I live, maintain a soldier's name.
> I'll purse it, I: the Highway is my Hope!
> His heart's not great that fears a little rope.

Hiding away from cities and supported by secret loyal sympathisers, a generation of highwaymen was still known by military rank – it could not raise a fresh army to overthrow Cromwell, but it could take satisfaction in robbing Parliamentarians, and there were many stories of Royalists who held up and humiliated their old enemies.

The tales that have survived seem always to emphasise gallantry and good humour, and make light of the robbery. London's highwaymen waylaid their victims on the heaths and commons just beyond the capital, where the main roads were bordered by ample natural cover for an ambush, and there was little danger of interruption. Hounslow Heath, the site now covered by Heathrow Airport, was notoriously dangerous for travellers from the west, though one favourite tale told how a quick-witted traveller was able to foil a holdup.

When challenged on the road, the victim seemed ready enough to hand over his money, but first he protested that if his family knew that he had been robbed without putting up a fight, he would be a laughing-stock – could the highwayman oblige him, perhaps, by firing his pistols through the crown of his hat? The hat could then be shown to prove how bravely he had resisted, how close he had come to death. Flattered by this tribute to his marksmanship, the highway emptied his pistols to make neat holes in the raised hat, only to find that he was staring down the barrel of a cocked pistol which the traveller had been concealing under his coat. The highwayman spurred his horse into a swift retreat.

All the stories of gallantry and good humour could not hide the truth that many highwaymen were brutal robbers and rapists, and that even the witty and courtly ones died squalid deaths at a rope's end, usually when still very young. The profession which promised rich rewards to the daring was a deathtrap for amateurs, and the short career of Joseph Picken was not unusual.

Picken was a respectable man who met and married a Billingsgate barmaid. At first they prospered when he became the landlord of a tavern in Windsor, but his wife proved extravagant, and was helped to spend by her mother. In debt, and reduced to cheap lodgings after losing his job, Picken despaired, and asked his wife what he should do.

'Do? Why, what should a man do that wants money and has any courage, but go upon the highway?'

Poor henpecked Picken was a thorough failure as a criminal, too – within a week of his first robbery he had been caught, tried, and condemned to death. The spendthrift Mrs Picken would have nothing more to do with him, but Picken bore no malice; he confessed all his sins, forgave his wife all, and on the road to his execution 'behaved himself with amazing circumstances of quietness and resignation.' There must have been as many Pickens as Turpins.

A GALLERY OF HIGHWAYMEN

Dick Turpin

The most famous of them all, Dick Turpin's reputation was created not by the man himself, but by Victorian versions of his life, which added a romantic flavour to the story of a successful but coarse criminal.

The real Turpin was born in 1705, the son of an Essex farmer, who was apprenticed to a London butcher, married young to an innkeeper's daughter, and first broke the law by stealing cattle to help his business. His next move was to rob smugglers on the coast by pretending to be a Revenue man, but when both the smugglers and the Customs officers hunted him he hid out in Epping Forest, where he fell in with a gang of deer poachers.

This gang turned to burglary, but their persistent robberies and rapes led in the end to the posting of large rewards and the capture and execution of three of them. It was then, in 1735, that Turpin discovered highway robbery, and the public discovered Turpin, who was unusually bold in his thefts.

An attempted robbery on the road to Cambridge led to a notorious partnership. Turpin held up a lone traveller who laughed out loud, crying 'What, dog eat dog? Come, come, brother Turpin, if you don't know me, I know you, and shall be glad of your company.' This intended victim was in fact Tom King, another famous highwayman, and the two men went into business together. Their base was a cave in Epping Forest large enough to hold themselves and their horses, a hideout which Turpin may have known since his poaching days, and where they were secretly brought food and supplies by Turpin's wife.

In 1737 the cave was discovered, and in fleeing the highwaymen killed the man who found them; still worse, King was seized by the landlord of an Epping tavern, and in trying to free him Turpin accidentally shot King dead. Working alone, Turpin continued to rob for some months longer but chose in the end to leave the London area, and while passing himself off as a reputable dealer, was arrested in York for stealing horses. By chance his true identity was discovered, he was convicted and sentenced to hang; he met death bravely, throwing himself from the ladder before a large crowd at Knavesmire.

Though he never owned a horse called Black Bess, and made no daredevil ride to York, the ordinary brutality of his crimes has been quite forgotten. For all this, Dick Turpin became the hero of novels and ballads, the most famous of all the highwaymen, perhaps because he had an unusually long career. When he went to the gallows in 1739 he was thirty-four years old, and had been a known working criminal for at least ten years: this in itself was an achievement, and he had become famous in his own time for his daring. The makers of the Turpin legend simply added qualities of chivalry and generosity borrowed from more attractive thieves of the time.

Claude Duval

> *Here lies Du Vall: Reader, if Male thou art,*
> *Look to thy purse: if Female, to thy heart.*
> *Much havoc has he made of both; for all*
> *Men he made stand, and women he made fall.*
> *The second Conquerer of the Norman race,*
> *Knights to his arms did yield, and Ladies to his face.*
> *Old Tyburn's glory: England's illustrious thief,*
> *Du Vall, the Ladies' Joy; Du Vall, the Ladies' grief.*
> The epitaph of Claude Duval,
> St Paul's Church, Covent Garden

Duval was the very model of the dashing gallant, 'an eternal feather in the cap of highway gentility', and responsible for much of the highwayman's reputation for courtesy. He was a Frenchman – from Normandy, as the rhyme reminds us – who had taken service with an exiled English Royalist in Paris, and came to England at the Restoration of Charles II in 1660.

The most famous of his exploits was to dance with a lady whose carriage he had brought to a halt on Hounslow Heath. To show that she was unafraid, she had taken out a flageolet – a small pipe – and played a

CLAUDE DUVAL DANCES A CORANTO
The French highwayman gained an exotic and romantic reputation, and society ladies donned masks to sneak a look at his body when it lay in state after his execution.

This fanciful picture shows the most famous exploit of the legendary Duval, when he paused during a robbery to invite a lady to dance with him on Hampstead Heath, but the real Duval was a brutal thief and rapist.

tune upon it; Duval in turn played well on a pipe drawn from his own pocket, then invited her to join him in dancing a coranto.

The gentle thief, the romantic seducer, was captured in a drunken stupor in a tavern called the Hole in the Wall near Covent Garden, to be hanged at Tyburn when he was just twenty-seven. His friends took his body to lie in state in a bar-room, and it is said that many ladies of quality dressed in black to come and pay their last respects.

Sixteen-string Jack

Jack Rann was a dandy and a showman, who gained his nickname for the silk string he tied to his breeches, and his fame for the many times he was arrested but acquitted.

Rann was no gentleman by birth, but began respectably enough as a servant and coachman. At twenty he found that his tastes were too expensive to be supported by honest toil, and after an unsatisfactory start as a pickpocket chose to equip himself as a highwayman, with a horse, a brace of pistols, and a fine suit of clothes. 'He was straight,' said

SIXTEEN-STRING JACK
The fresh, informal sketch reminds us that this notorious highwayman died young, after a flamboyant but very brief career, the Billy the Kid or Ned Kelly of his time.

one contemporary, 'of a genteel carriage and made a very handsome appearance.'

First arrested in 1772, he was captured and acquitted five more times within the next two years, to the frustration of the Bow Street Runners, though he made no secret of his work and made a point of flaunting his new and expensive clothes in the most fashionable places. He ran up large debts, and robbed to pay them off, defying the Runners to stop him. His technique was always to rob in a shabby disguise, and trust that no witness would be able to identify the dandy in court, but inevitably he was at last convicted.

After a last riotous round of drinking parties in Newgate, including a dinner for just himself and seven of his favourite girls, Rann went to

Tyburn dressed in a new pea-green suit. Though he was no apologist for criminals, even Dr Johnson found something admirable in Rann: praising Thomas Gray he declared that the poet 'towered above the ordinary run of verse as Sixteen string Jack above the ordinary footpad.'

THE BURGLARS

When Willie Sutton, a famous American safecracker and hold-up man was asked why he robbed banks, he gave the obvious reply – 'That's where the money is!'

Thieves have always followed this golden rule, and adapted their crimes to exploit the possibilities of their time and their city. Willie's eighteenth-century ancestors became highwaymen, to seize wealth when it took to the road. Profitable burglary came later.

Until just a couple of centuries ago, there were only two sorts of house – the well-protected few with real wealth in them, and the very many which held little of value. Walking around London, or any British town today with a burglar's eye, we can see this for ourselves. At the centre are the few houses of the old rich, and perhaps a picturesque sample of homes which belonged to the poor of the eighteenth century and earlier; then, moving outwards, comes a ring of Georgian houses, then usually a broader band of Victorian mansions and villas, like the rings of a tree. Each band shows the prosperity of the next generation, and the wider hunting ground for the professional burglar.

Two or three hundred years ago there was a simple structure to society, one so old that it seemed it must last forever. The wealthy – landowners, merchants and professional people such as doctors and lawyers – lived in their mansions and town houses attended by servants, and their possessions were distinctive: since they commissioned their furniture and their jewellery the goods were too easily identified to sell on in safety. They bought on account, making little day-to-day use of cash, and were quite difficult to rob. A burglar might try to subvert a maid or a manservant to get entry to a house, and hope to make off with silver plate which could quickly be melted down to render it anonymous, but it was a hazardous business. In those divided days most burglaries of houses and shops were trifling – the poor stealing from the poor – and yielded little more than the price of a glass or two of gin.

Then the Industrial Revolution, the sudden vast growth of industry and trade, created new classes. Across the country there were now clerks and managers, small manufacturers, middleman merchants and more new professionals who were prosperous but lived much more modestly than the old rich.

London had always had a trading class, but now the City was growing fast to accommodate the subcontractors, the book keepers, all the many small proprietors and agents. They lived in newly built smaller houses and employed just a few servants, and not all of these would sleep in the house. Their possessions were not mass-produced in the modern sense, but were no longer rare pieces of fine craftsmanship. They were ready to be burgled, and just the ancient watchmen and the few dozen Bow Street Runners stood between the crooks and their prey.

To make the task easier still, that same technology which was creating the new industrial wealth also provided the tools and techniques for a new kind of thief. Cheaper steel made fortunes for the entrepreneurs of the West Midlands, in an industry which depended on thousands of small workshops. But among the craftsmen who worked by day as lawful subcontractors were many who would ask no questions if a stranger called at night to order a specialised drill, a jackscrew, or a set of levers which could be folded or dismantled.

The new boosted trade demanded new forms of money. Where the landowner might receive his tenants' rents once a year, and settle his own bills no more often, the merchants needed cash for supplies and wages, credit to cover advance orders, easier ways to carry money with them as they travelled. To replace clumsy gold coin, banks issued many more pieces of paper – bills of exchange, notes of credit – which could be used as cash. The financial needs of industry fulfilled the dreams of the working criminal, as vulnerable households and businesses filled with the kind of wealth that could be carried far away, then sold with ease. By 1800, burglary was the most profitable criminal trade of them all: less than one highway robbery in ten yielded £10 or more, but a quarter of burglaries reached that figure.

Burglary – the new crime

Of course there had always been burglaries, but the vast expansion of opportunity brought more than simple growth in numbers. Here was a new specialist criminal trade and the opening of an intriguing arms race.

Burglary is a crime of stealth rather than strength, and needs patience and planning, coolness under pressure. It is easy to contrast the ideal burglar with the ideal highwayman, footpad or pickpocket, his rivals as criminal specialists. The highwayman depended on a bold courage to intimidate his victims so thoroughly that they neither fought him nor felt it safe to flee. It is hardly surprising that the work appealed to men who had held military commands.

The footpad might hope to achieve the same domination, but was ready to move straight to the use of force, killing if necessary. The pickpocket needed to be physically nimble, dextrous, and willing to put himself at risk in a crowded street where he might be seized if discovered. It was often work for children who could get close to a mark unnoticed, then flee while clumsy adults floundered.

Burglary needed new skills and techniques, but it also demanded a new type of courage, of the slow-burning kind that made it possible to work quietly and persistently as patrolling watchmen passed by, as householders slept; the ideal burglary was one which would not be discovered until many hours after the thief had left. There were rewards for co-operation – methods of breaking in had to be learned, the bigger jobs needed teamwork and mutual trust.

Beating the burglar

The new homes and businesses used a defence which had always to be overcome or bypassed – the lock. There had always been cheap, crude locks and expensive, elaborate locks. Now the new metalworking industry was making cheap and solid locks to fit street doors, cabinets and stores. Luckily for the burglars, the mechanism inside almost all the new locks was to an old and pickable pattern – the servant tempted to pilfer might be frustrated, but not the working burglar who took the time to learn some basic skills.

By the 1780s burglary had reached crimewave levels, and furious householders demanded action. The creaky old system of patrolling watchmen was not protecting them, and there were too many thieves for the few dozen Bow Street Runners to catch. The only thing that property owners could do was to improve the security of their own homes and businesses: there was suddenly a market for better locks, and hot competition to design and produce them.

The first big breakthrough was announced in 1787, when this notice appeared in a London shop window beneath a strange new cylindrical lock:

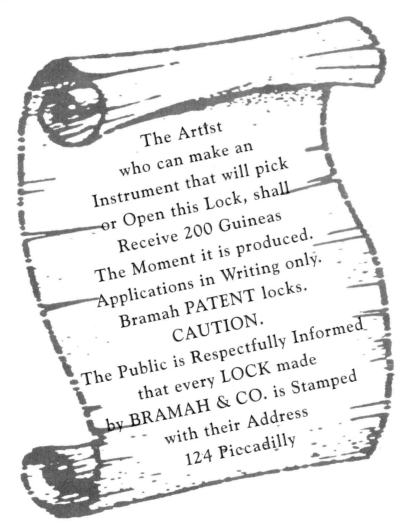

The Artist
who can make an
Instrument that will pick
or Open this Lock, shall
Receive 200 Guineas
The Moment it is produced.
Applications in Writing only.
Bramah PATENT locks.
CAUTION.
The Public is Respectfully Informed
that every LOCK made
by BRAMAH & CO. is Stamped
with their Address
124 Piccadilly

Many tried, but no one was able to pick that lock and claim the prize for sixty-four years. The importance of the lock was not its design: it worked well, but it was unnecessarily complex and required a great deal of hand finishing during manufacture. Much more important was that Bramah's commercial success stimulated inventors and investors to devise, produce and sell locks to the same market. Hundreds of patents were applied for, dozens of new locks were offered for sale.

Of course, the effect of all this was to make the craft of burgling even more important. As more and more wealth was protected by the new locks, so the successful thief needed greater technical knowledge and skill. Breaking and entering might once have needed no more than a jemmy and a couple of pieces of bent metal, but now the tool kits of working burglars could run to more than a hundred cleverly made tools. The successful burglar was a technological whizzkid, the computer hacker of his day: he not only had secret skills but was able to steal much more wealth than any street robber, and became, as one writer put it 'chief among the fraternity of thieves'.

Bizarre burglary

Among the oddest burglaries on record was a housebreaking in 1829 for which James Bell was charged with stealing a shirt, a worsted comforter, and a body. A lodging-house keeper called Daniel Redday had offered a room to a man who died suddenly; while waiting for a coroner's jury to examine the corpse, he had laid it out in his back room, clothed in the shirt and the comforter. That very night, Redday was alarmed to hear noises from the room where the body lay, and instead of going upstairs to take a look, he ran from the house. Outside, he spotted immediately that a ladder had been put up against the wall, and that four men were standing on it. When he went to grab the ladder, Redday somehow tipped it over, and five men fell to the ground – five living, one dead. Three of the bodysnatchers managed to escape, but the luckless Bell was captured, convicted, and sentenced to transportation for life.

Going equipped to steal

If we rummaged through the many extra pockets sewn inside the long coat of an old-time burglar, we would find some tools known to any carpenter – a stout hammer, a mallet, a saw and a gimlet or two – and several which were familiar but adapted. These might include broad-bladed drillbits, fitted to a stock which broke down easily into several smaller components, steel shafts which plugged together to form crowbars of varying lengths, each with one end curved, the other sharpened like a chisel.

These might almost be the tools of a legitimate but eccentric craftsman. Less easy to explain away, for all but a locksmith, would be the lock-opening devices: spread out in wallets like the tools of a surgeon, we would find a wide selection of skeleton keys and key blanks on large rings (usually wrapped tightly to stop them jingling), more keys and odd hooked wires called picklocks; next to all these, a selection of shortened rat-tail files, ready to cut the blanks for a precise fit.

The last items were the most obviously criminal: a tiny lantern with a shrouded lens, a folding ladder, a revolver, handcuffs, and a small bottle of poison – prussic acid or nux vomica to silence watchdogs.

The burglar would have served an apprenticeship to use such a kit, until he could use it swiftly and silently in the dark by touch alone; he would have invested a great deal of his money in buying all the parts, and would treat them with a craftsman's respect, keeping good sharp edges and oiling them against rust.

On the job

Faced with a lock, our burglar could try to open it or work around it. A first peek through the keyhole would show whether a key had been left in the lock from the inside, perhaps to prevent picking. To find a key was good luck – among his tools was a small but powerful long-nosed vice which could be pushed into the keyhole and screw-tightened on the tip of the key, then steadily turned to unlock the door.

If there were no key, almost all locks could be opened with one of a small kit of L- and Z-shaped skeleton keys. If it still wouldn't yield, the burglar might choose a key blank that was a good close fit, ready coated with a thin layer of wax; when inserted and turned, the blank would show clearly the imprint of the wards within the lock, and could be cut on the spot to fit. For any lock that would not yield, or to tackle a bolt, the burglar would pluck out and assemble his drill, to make a ring of holes in the wooden panel, then join the drill holes with his keyhole saw to make an aperture big enough to put in his hand and reach the fastening from inside. If the door were nailed shut or fastened tight, the entire panel could be cut out in the same way to let the burglar squeeze through.

Once inside, the burglar would swiftly establish escape routes, unfastening another door or window ready to flee, and fasten his entry door by tapping a wedge under it. Then if any passer-by saw signs of the break-in, he would find the door shut against him, and the burglar could continue his work knowing that any attempt to follow him in would be noisy and delayed.

Our man now had to find money or objects of value, but he would probably have chosen this house because he had some indication of what there was, and where it was. He might have a detailed description from a treacherous servant, or gossip from a chimneysweep or delivery boy; for business premises, he might have made a visit himself in working hours, on some pretext that had given him a chance to look around.

To open a drawer or a cupboard required only steady pressure from a jemmy; a simple metal box would probably split with a blow from the hammer – to keep the noise down, the burglar would strike through a pad of leather. Stronger boxes would yield to wedges hammered into the space around the door or lid, starting with thin ones and working up to fat ones which would open a gap wide enough for a substantial jemmy to be inserted.

The great Cornhill safebreaking

Safes were not invented, but evolved from all the strongboxes and treasure chests that went before. When chests were made large and strong and heavy, their lids became too difficult and dangerous to lift, and it was logical to stand the box on its end. The first safes were made as the chests had been, from iron or oak reinforced with metal bands, but increased production made possible a simpler form which became standard.

From the end of the eighteenth century, when safes went into large-scale production, the conventional design used a framework of angled iron to which sheets of iron were rivetted. Such safes could be easily made in a range of sizes, used standard stock, and needed only the limited skills and equipment found in all the small workshops of the West Midlands. Even the most reputable manufacturers bought safes from the subcontractors, adding only their locks and their nameplates.

Early safes looked strong, and certainly gave better protection than any wooden structure, but burglars found that their old methods would still work with just a little more effort. The iron cladding of the safes was soft, and could be cut with a hammer and chisel, or parted from the rivets which held it in place. The last great triumph of this muscle-powered safebreaking, a crime that shook London in the 1860s as much as the Great Train Robbery startled the country in the 1960s, was the Cornhill burglary.

The victim of the theft was John Walker. Mr Walker was a jeweller in Cornhill, in the City of London, and to protect his valuable stock he had taken every sensible precaution: his shop was on a busy street, and he kept gas lamps lit through the night so that passing police patrols could look into the shop, through the peepholes cut in the strong shutters. The rooms inside had been lined with iron, and as his last and best defence Mr Walker had invested in a Milner's Quadruple Patent Violence, Robbery and Fraud-resisting Safe. There was even a mirror fixed so that every approach to the safe was clearly visible.

Businessmen were rattled in early 1865: thieves in Manchester and London had committed a series of daring shop burglaries, and there seemed to be nothing that would stop them. The thoroughness of Mr Walker's defences made it all the more shocking to discover that on Monday 6 February 'The safe had been burst open, and all the most valuable portion of Mr Walker's stock ... gold watches, chronometers, diamond rings, pins, studs, bracelets, earrings ... and the cash-box, containing a quantity of gold and some valuable securities, was gone.' Mr Walker had lost a total of £6000.

There was panic: hurried meetings, impassioned pleas to the authorities, criticisms of the City Police, above all a dread that no business was now secure. A typical editorial began: 'Now that the enemy applies the principles of war to the acquisition of gold and jewels it is time to devise defensive plans even more scientific than those already adopted.'

In fact the thieves were soon captured, and it turned out that they had used no new wonder weapon, but had worked conscientiously through the weekend with simple tools. The full story came out in a remarkable way: the principal safecracker, a flamboyant young man called Caseley, became Mr Walker's most helpful witness when he sued the safemakers for selling him an inadequate box.

Caseley came to court in his prison uniform to give a performance which became the talk of the town, full of fascinating details of criminal methods and underworld slang. Mr Walker lost his case, but the new public awareness of the threat of burglary gave the lock- and safemaking trades a tremendous boost.

THE PIRATE

Like the highwayman on land, the pirate is often a romantic figure, the bold sea-rover who led a cut-throat crew to seize rich prizes on the Spanish Main. There were ruthless and evil pirates like the rascally Blackbeard, hunted for their cruelties and strung up from the yardarm; there were heroic, patriotic pirates like Sir Francis Drake, scourge of the enemies of his queen. But which was the famous Captain Kidd?

Captain William Kidd, an experienced middle-aged sea-captain, was commissioned by a number of very prominent men to lead an expedition. It was a business venture from which the Lord Chancellor, the First Lord of the Admiralty, and the Secretary of State – the king himself had wanted a share, but had been unable to raise the money – all hoped to see a rich profit from their investment of £6000 in a ship called the *Adventure*.

Kidd's mission was 'to seize and take pirates and to bring them to justice'; he was certainly expected to capture pirates, but his most important task was to take back their plunder. The original plan had been to tackle pirates in the Red Sea, but since England and France were at war, he was also entitled to attack any French ships he encountered. Such enterprises were common, but Kidd's backers were greedier than most and would allow the crew, who received no other pay, to keep only one quarter of the plunder.

Kidd set sail in 1695 from London to New York, where he took on more crew, then made his way to Madagascar. He was able to capture several French prizes, but not before unrest at the poor plunder had caused a minor mutiny and the death of one of the hands. He seemed luckier in seizing the *Queddah Merchant*, a large ship with a rich cargo which he took for his own, burning the *Adventure* and setting off for the West Indies.

He left his prize with a man called Button, and returned to New York to find that Button had sailed ahead of him and accused him of piracy. The colonial governor ordered his arrest, and when political opponents of the expedition's sponsors saw a chance for mischief, a Parliamentary motion was passed that Kidd, and all the documents and depositions in the case, should be sent to London.

On his return, Kidd was first brought to the Bar of the House of Commons, in the hope that he would incriminate his employers. Although he made a very poor impression by a display of drunkenness, Kidd said nothing which implicated them, and was sent to the Old Bailey for ordinary criminal trial. His defence was that he had seized ships which, although not French, were carrying French passes (and were thus legitimate spoils of war) and that he had already handed over these passes when he was arrested in New York.

The court could find no passes, decided that they did not exist, and condemned Kidd and an accomplice to death. As was the custom for pirates they were to be hanged at Execution Dock rather than Tyburn. At the first attempt to execute him the rope around Kidd's neck broke and he fell to the ground alive, but a fresh rope was soon brought and the hanging completed.

Captain Kidd was hanged on 23 May 1701. More than two hundred years later a researcher in the Public Records Office in London found the missing French passes which would have proved his innocence.

THE PICKPOCKETS

The sun is bright, and John Bull is in a fine mood as he walks down a lively London street, pauses to hear another verse of a busker's bawdy ballad, flinches when a dog on a piece of string makes a sudden barking lunge at him, but is reassured when the owner apologises; he yells a warning to a small boy who seems about to run into his legs, but succeeds in catching an arm and steering him safely to one side; the child then collides with a young woman carrying a basket, she trips, and is grateful to Bull and the other three men who help her to her feet.

Bull is ready for his lunch, but when he reaches the tavern door, a rude oaf lunges ahead of him, and curses him when he protests; for a moment Bull thinks that he is to be struck, but another man trying to enter becomes impatient at the delay, and shouts back at the bully, who shrugs and goes on his way; grateful, Bull offers his saviour a drink, but the gracious fellow declines the offer. When Bull comes to pay for his meal, he finds that his purse, his watch and his handkerchief have all been stolen.

Question

Who robbed John Bull?

Answer

Any of them, perhaps all of them. The balladeer, the dog-owner, the boy, the girl, the passers-by, the bully, the helper – each was an established role in the dramatic routine for a working pickpocket. Even the dog might be a suspect – a man called Tom Gerard taught his dog to steal from pockets.

Picking pockets was a trade in which hundreds made a day-to-day living. An ambitious novice with some natural aptitude would be offered the training and development of an apprenticeship; once this was successfully completed, the new member of the craft could draw on the knowledge and professional co-operation of fellow thieves. For the most profitable work a closed shop was vigorously enforced, and from among the many who were no more than competent a very few proved that they could transcend mere craftsmanship and achieve the status and rewards of the artist.

Crime follows wealth. When it was still common for a man to carry the cash he needed to make a purchase, or the proceeds of an important sale, all the several kinds of street thief had plans to empty his purse. He might be suddenly assaulted, even killed – a quick but risky robbery. He might be lured by a trick into handing his money over willingly, but this required time, and powers of persuasion not given to all.

Picking pockets was a workmanlike middle path for a professional. It combined physical skill, even forcefulness, with a degree of applied intelligence, to prepare and see through an encounter which was a bold theft, but unnoticed by its victim.

The performance of each theft was a little like a music hall turn, either as a sketch for several players, or a solo act of great virtuosity. Like a stage routine, the appearance of spontaneity was achieved by long, hard rehearsal until each player knew the character and the movements well. Like Punch and Judy, some of these playlets had a long classical tradition, each performance only a slight adaptation of the last.

From Norman times there have been girls of modest and virtuous appearance needing assistance, bullies sent packing by a friendly passer-by, and an endless army of stumbling clumsy drunks. The techniques of

LOCK-UP AT THE
POLICE OFFICE
*Here is a fine collection of
the Regency low life of
London – all the drunks and
scroungers, rogues and
ladies of the night swept up
to appear before the
magistrates in the morning.*

distraction are pure showbiz, and are still used by illusionists – why else do they have glamorous assistants? – and even film stunt men. Watch how many times the stunt men spill props during staged falls: each man needs to make a controlled drop, and as he tumbles he will throw an armful of papers or a tray of glasses into the air. We can't help it: our eyes follow the flying glasses, not the skilled way in which he used his hands and arms to soften his landing.

Like magicians, pickpockets depended on their combination of manual skill and clever well-timed distraction, both to carry out the theft and to cover their retreat. In the example above, if John Bull had slapped his pocket at the door of the tavern, and in a moment of sudden realisation turned to accuse his saviour, that man would have allowed himself to be searched without any fear. Bull's purse would already have been carried off by an accomplice. From among all the common-or-garden street thieves some pickpockets rose to star billing, to join the highest levels of the criminal aristocracy – well-dressed men whose manners were refined enough to pass in the politest society, who lived in fashionable town houses with servants, carriages and all the appearance of legitimate prosperity. They existed in every age, but were prominent enough in Victorian times for them to be given a title – these were the 'swell mobsmen', and it was said that to achieve this status a pickpocket had to have learned the elements of his craft before his voice broke.

TEN POUNDS
REWARD,
Borough Compter, 11th April, 1825.

WHEREAS,
JOHN MAHONEY,
Confined under a Charge of Felony, Escaped from this Prison early this Morning,

He is about 14 years of Age, Four feet five and a half inches in height, dark complexion, dark eyes, dark hair, round features, born of Irish Parents; had on when he went away a common slop-made blue jacket, blue trowsers, with black horn buttons.   He has been four times at Brixton for Petty Larceny.

Whoever may apprehend the said **JOHN MAHONEY,** and will lodge him in any of his Majesty's Gaols, shall receive the above Reward, by applying to the Keeper of the said Prison.

Robins & Sons, Printers, 57, Tooley Street.

These were men who would adopt an appropriate disguise for any setting or occasion, masquerading as clergymen and courtiers, business-men and bankers. Their lives were as controlled by the seasons and social calendar as those of the nobility and gentry on whom they preyed: they were in the best enclosures at Ascot and Epsom, bought tickets for the most fashionable balls and music festivals, joined the crowds at political meetings.

These high-society gatecrashers were astonishingly daring: at the end of the eighteenth century one of the most impressive performers, Henry Sterne – 'Gentleman Harry' – penetrated St James' Palace on at least two occasions. With a small band of well-dressed confederates he tried to steal from the Prince of Wales, and on another occasion he was arrested, dressed in a Court suit, having stolen the pendant of the Order of the Garter from the neck of the Duke of Beaufort. Sterne had a rival in George Barrington, whose speciality was to patrol Covent Garden dressed as a clergyman – he managed to lift a diamond-studded gold snuff box from the pocket of Prince Orloff.

Picking pockets took much longer to learn than the cruder skills of robbery, and when young boys were sent to reformatories and schools instead of prison, the real-life Fagins lost their recruits.

CRIMINAL CALLINGS - THE WORDS OF THE UNDERWORLD

The underworld has always had a secret and safe language: working crooks invent words and phrases which no respectable bystander will understand. We use words like 'filch' and 'slang' itself, which came from the criminal vocabulary, but of course as soon as each word becomes commonly known, it has to be replaced.

From time to time interested scholars have recorded the criminal slang of their time, and the lists and lexicons they compiled give us a detailed picture of life among the thieves and swindlers in town, on the road and in prison.

Strangely, these lists give us knowledge that would otherwise have been lost. When there were neither newspapers nor detailed court records, only the most dramatic and unusual crimes were described in print, but by writing down all the many specialised words that criminals themselves used, they have let us know just how common thieves and rogues actually worked. Here is a selection, chosen because the words are both colourful and revealing:

Abraham	A beggar who deceived passers-by with a show of madness.
academy buzz-napper	An apprentice pickpocket.
accident lurk	A deception used by beggars who pretended that a terrible accident had befallen them or their families.
amusers	Street robbers who filled their pockets with dust, which they threw into the eyes of their victims, so that an accomplice could rob them.
anglers	Thieves who used a pole and line, just like a fisherman, to steal cloth and clothing through open windows – the most skilful were even said to have lifted the bedclothes off sleeping householders.
ark ruffian	River villains who conspired with crooked watermen: while out on the river, they would pick a fight with a fellow passenger, rob and strip him, and throw him overboard to die.
barnacle	One of a team of tavern conmen who would rig a card game to fleece a 'coney' (meaning rabbit, i.e. the victim). The barnacle would enter the inn, where his partner the 'verser' was already established, pretending to be a stranger. Though it was the barnacle who suggested a game, his role was to lose enough money to tempt the coney in, until he could be brought to one last losing bet.
bat-fowler	Pretending that he had dropped a gold piece or a valuable ring in the street at night, the bat-fowler would call into a shop and ask to borrow the only candle. As he searched outside, accomplices would slip into the shop

	to steal what they could.
black-spice racket	Robbing chimneysweeps of their bags of soot.
blue pigeon flyer	A thief who pretended to be a plumber (literally a lead worker) who would inspect the state of a roof, but then stole the lead ('blue pigeon') by wrapping it around his body.
buttock and twang	A colourful old name for a classic crime: a victim would be lured into a quiet spot by a woman, but then robbed by her partner.
cat and kitten sneaking	A petty crime: stealing quart and pint pewter pots from taverns.
chiving lay	A 'chiv' was a knife, and a chiving lay was a theft which involved cutting. Valuables such as buckles and watches might be sliced from the clothing of the victim; more elaborately a knife might be used to cut the straps holding up the body of a coach – then, as the coachman stopped to survey the damage, any handy boxes or goods could be stolen.
cock-a-brass	No more than a man who stood outside an inn used for confidence tricks or robbery. If a victim chased out after the thieves, the cock-a-brass would send him in the wrong direction. It was simple work for the sick, the elderly and the simple-minded.
cross-biting cully	Cross-biting was cheating, especially cheating other crooks, and a cross-biting cully was usually skilled with false dice.
curbing law	Rather like angling, curbing law was the theft of goods through windows, using a long pole with a hook on the end.
cygaret	A thief who went to churches and other public places, and simply cut away parts of his victims' clothing (lace and good cloth were valuable).
dimber damber	Dimber meant handsome, damber meant rascal: a dimber damber was the chief of a gang of thieves.

dining-room post Before stamps were introduced in 1840, it was the person receiving a letter who paid the postage. The thief would arrive at a lodging-house pretending to be a postman, and wait downstairs while the landlady took his letters up to her lodgers. Left alone in the dining room, the thief stole anything to hand.

dobbin rig A way of stealing valuable ribbons: the thief would arrive early at a shop when only an apprentice was working, sit in the darkest corner, and demand to see a great assortment from which she would choose. While keeping the apprentice busy with requests for more light, or scissors, the thief was able to tuck away yards and yards of ribbon into a secret pocket.

fawney rig A classic cheat in which the rogue discreetly dropped a purse in the street. When a passer-by picked up the purse, he would find inside a ring (the fawney) which appeared to be valuable. The rogue would claim a share in the find, but allow himself to be bought out of it for a modest sum. Thinking that he was getting a good deal, the victim paid off the rogue, only to find later that the ring was almost worthless. This was such a common crime that there was a large shop which specialised in selling suitable rings.

fogle-hunter A pickpocket who specialised in stealing handkerchiefs.

freshwater mariner Rogues who pretended to have been shipwrecked or robbed by pirates, and claimed to be on their way back to their home ports. This story was used to gain sympathy as they begged, and was usually supported by false documents; as one writer noted, 'their ships were drowned on Salisbury Plain'.

glimmering mort	A mort was a woman; a glimmering mort told elaborate lies about losing her home and fortune in a fire.
high-toby gloak	The high-toby was the main road, and a high-toby gloak was therefore a highwayman.
hook-pole lay	This was a technique used by footpads who used a hooked staff to drag riders from their horses, then robbed them.
knap a jacob	The night soil men who emptied toilets used to carry a ladder on their carts. While the men left the cart to go into a house and empty the privy, thieves would take their ladder (the jacob) to use it in a burglary.
little snakesman	A tiny boy trained to enter a house by the smallest opening, then open a door for the thieves to enter. When they had finished, the boy would lock the door, and make a wriggled exit; the advantage of leaving the door locked was that servants were usually blamed for the theft.
lully-priggers	Thieves who took linen left hanging out to dry; worse, thieves who robbed children of their clothing.
magsmen	Well-dressed Victorian swindlers who preyed upon visitors from the country, often disguised as clergymen or nobility.
mat macer	Very simply, a thief who went round in the early morning when servants were beating household mats and carpets, to steal any that were unattended.
peter-hunting	Stealing boxes and trunks from coaches; a peter meant any sturdy box, and so went on to mean a safe, and finally a prison cell.
pricking in the wicker for a dolphin	This elaborate phrase described the theft of loaves from bakers' baskets when they were in public houses.
pudding-snammer	A thief who stole from a cook-shop.
reader merchant	A pickpocket who specialised in lifting pocket-books.

red sail-yard docker	A thief who made a living by stealing stores from the royal dockyards.
resurrection rig	The stealing of bodies from graves, for sale to anatomists.
royal scamp	A highwayman who robbed without violence, and stole only from those who seemed wealthy enough to bear the loss.
rum dragger	A thief on horseback who pretended to be drunk and staggered into a collision with a waggon carrying packages; then, saying he was too drunk to ride further, he offered the waggoneer money to lead his horse, and allow him to sleep off his drink in the back of the cart. Once on the cart, he relabelled any packages that looked valuable. When the waggon arrived at its next stop, an accomplice would claim the relabelled packages.
running rumbler	One of a team of pickpockets, the running rumbler would roll a large grindstone along the pavement. Afraid that their toes would be run over, passers-by jumped out of the way, and in the great confusion their pockets could easily be picked.
running snavel	Lying in wait to steal school-books and food from small boys.
shoful-pitcher	A passer of counterfeit money.
sky-farmer	Beggars who carried forged documents pretending that they were gentlemen farmers who had been ruined by fire or other disaster.
slang mort play	A trick by women who pretended to be pregnant and in pain, to gain entry to a house where they could then steal.
sneeze-lurker	A thief who threw snuff into a victim's face, then robbed him.
snotter-hauler	Specialised pickpocket who stole handkerchiefs.

tinny-hunter	Thief who went to fires, and pretended to help the victims, but stole their property.
tolliban rig	Another begging deceit: a well-dressed young woman would tie back her tongue with a piece of thread, and gain sympathy by pretending that she was dumb. Gesturing for a piece of paper to write a note, she would offer to tell fortunes.

Thieves might use just one successful technique for most of their lives – there was an endless supply of fresh countrymen who knew nothing of even the oldest tricks – but success and status in the underworld usually depended on serving an apprenticeship to learn the simpler methods, then rising to bigger bolder crimes such as highway robbery.

THE ROARING GIRL

Even in a colourful time, there was no more striking criminal in London than Moll Cutpurse. Swaggering in men's clothes, the pipe-smoking, hard-drinking Mary Frith was 'a very Tomrig and Rumple scuttle' – a tomboy – who turned down the conventional life of a maidservant to earn her famous nickname as a pickpocket, but rose to become an empress of crime.

The young Mary Frith was a torment to her respectable family. She was apprenticed to a saddler, but spent her time hanging around street corners with ruffians and ne'er-do-wells; when an attempt was made to send her abroad she jumped ship. While still in her teens she had enthusiastically taken to a life of low crime as a pickpocket and robber, and it seemed that young Mary must soon take the ride to the gallows. After all, she made no attempt to hide herself away – her outrageous behaviour ensured that she was recognised and remembered wherever she appeared.

In fact, her vivid character made her a heroine rather than a villain: she was as famous for her free-spending generosity as for her brawling bad temper. When still a young woman in her twenties, Moll inspired Middleton and Dekker to write a witty, vastly successful play called *The Roaring Girl*, which embellished all Moll's exploits and turned an eccentric criminal into a star.

This fictional Moll was said to have 'the spirit of four great parishes, and a voice that will drown all the city.' It is hard to imagine that any

See here the Prefideffe o'th pilfring Trade
Mercuryes fecond; Venus's onely Mayd
Doublet and breeches in a Uniform dreffe
The Female Humurrift a Kickfhaw meffe
Heres no attraction that your fancy greets
But if her FEATURES pleafe not read her FEATS.

Moll Cutpurse, in the portrait published soon after her death, is shown as the middle-aged highway robber she became, dressed in men's clothes and wearing a sword. The caption makes it clear that the reader was expected to see her as a bold heroine rather than a villain.

actress could match the boldness of the real Moll, who turned her punishment for one minor offence into a great public drama, as one writer recorded:

> Last Sunday, Moll Cutpurse, a notorious baggage, that used to go about in man's apparel, and challenged the field of diverse gallants, was brought to St Paul's Cross, where she wept bitterly and seemed very penitent. But it is since doubted she was maudlin drunk, being discovered to have tippled of three quarts of sack before she came to her penance.

It was the kind of fame which needs living up to, but it may have given Moll some protection: she was captured many times, branded and gaoled, but survived to die in old age, after a lifetime of richly varied crime. For all her broad crudity, Moll was no fool. She saw that while the careers of her fellow thieves were short, the fences – the receivers of stolen property – made great fortunes, and remained safe from arrest. With a fine business sense Moll opened a shop in a prominent position on Fleet Street where she could charge the highest prices, and it became famous as a well-run, straight-dealing bureau where victims could reliably recover items stolen from them.

Expanding still further, Moll ran a forging operation and created an academy of crime at which the mysteries of pickpocketing and criminal crafts were passed on to new generations, Moll herself acting as tutor. In her fifties she returned to stealing for herself, as a highwaywoman, apparently to enjoy the risk-taking rather than the profit.

Moll's most famous exploit on the road – even if it is not true, it is remarkable that it was believed when Moll was already more than sixty years old – was to hold up and shoot Fairfax, Cromwell's chief general, on Hounslow Heath. They said she made her escape by shooting two of his horses, and though captured, tried and condemned to death, she bought her way out of Newgate with a £200 bribe to her gaolers.

Sadly, although this brawling, tipsy, generous woman had a long life, she died just a year before the monarchy was restored. Like many who enjoyed what the killjoy Roundheads despised, she had been a staunch Royalist, and in her will left £20 to pay for a grand party to celebrate the king's return.

THE SMUGGLERS

> At dead of night a band of burly men, holding their swords to their sides for fear of making a noise which might alert the Excise men, tread softly down to the water's edge. Drawn by a shielded lantern, a heavily laden open boat drifts gently in, and strong hands seize the gunwhales. Guided by whispers and silent signals the gang brings ashore rich contraband, passing from hand to hand barrels of brandy, chests of tea and spices, rolls of fine cloth, until all are safely loaded onto waiting horses. With a last satisfied wave, the sailors bend to their oars, the boat slips away darkly on the tide; the smugglers are already melting into the night.

The scene at the water's edge is familiar from costume dramas and romantic films: the smugglers are appealing rural rogues with robust Cornish accents, led by the gallant swashbuckling hero who is no more criminal than any poacher who shoots the odd rabbit for his pot. History is less kind to the smugglers. The age of smuggling was the greatest period of organised crime in England, as vast and pervasive as all the operations of the Mafia. From the sailors bringing the goods from overseas, through the networks of distribution to the final seller, it was an industry which employed thousands.

Just as soon as any tax or duty was imposed, there was profit to be made from evading it, and some of the earliest smugglers were the 'owlers', whose contraband went out rather than in – their profit lay in avoiding export duties on English wool. The real boom came with the growth of colonies and plantations overseas and the popularity of new commodities such as tea, sugar and tobacco.

Greed made a market for smuggled goods, when the seventeenth century Trade and Navigation Acts gave British shipowners the monopoly of carrying and selling the produce of the American colonies. This privilege was greatly abused, and the Americans saw a poor return for the crops they grew, while paying high prices for any imports. Smugglers undercut the monopolists both ways, to bring goods in cheaply and obtain a market price for exports; they became heroes to the colonists, and the governors and officials of the colonies had every interest in protecting and assisting them.

Colonial trade promised easy money for the Crown as well as shippers. Governments had fewer ways of raising taxes, in the days before income and purchase taxes such as VAT: the new trade seemed to offer a chance to collect large sums of money very simply. Customs duties were so important as a source of funds that at the end of the eighteenth century half of all the civil servants in London were employed by the Excise.

The British seem to have become addicted to tea at the first sip, and although it began as a luxury, an indulgence of the upper classes, even the poor had started to drink great quantities of sweet tea in the eighteenth century, and in trying to capitalise on the obsession, governments insisted on setting the duty on tea particularly high. In 1733, when duty-paid tea was sold at five shillings per pound in England, the same tea was available for sixpence (ten per cent of that English price) in Holland: there were handsome profits for smugglers and their agents, and to avoid such heavy duties even the most respectable people thought nothing of buying their tea on the black market. By 1784 Pitt calculated that of the thirteen million pounds of tea consumed in Britain each year, duty had been paid on less than half that amount.

As for tea and tobacco, so for wine and brandy, sugar and silk; another contemporary estimate claimed that one third of all British trade with France and with Holland was in smuggled goods. To move all the contraband demanded an enormous workforce: when the population of the entire kingdom was just eight million, fully twenty thousand people were occupied full-time in the trade. Many times that number acted as occasional porters and part-time traders; so many men left the land to join the smuggling networks that farmers could hardly compete, and there were shortages of labour in some counties.

London and smuggling

Different routes were employed for different merchandise, with the bulkier tea, brandy and wine most usually brought within range of a suitable coast and then offloaded in smaller boats, while tobacco and silks were usually brought directly to ports such as London. In London there had been few wharves until Tudor times, and it was long the practice to moor a ship in midstream and offload into boats and lighters. Elizabeth I ordered that ships should discharge their cargoes only at specified 'Legal Quays', but these were too few to handle all the traffic, and ships still spent a long time at anchor in the Pool of London: smuggling captains had only to arrange for their loads to be 'stolen' during this waiting period.

Further variations included a common method which took advantage of the low duties payable on tobacco brought in for re-export. The ship would enter London, duty would be paid in full, then a rebate obtained as the vessel set sail once more, but instead of leaving the country it would offload further down the Thames, or on the Medway, and the tobacco would soon be on its way back down the road to the capital.

These methods were normal for larger and frequent loads, but there were any number of smaller operations. Diplomats from many countries used their official status to protect lucrative shipments of tea and coffee; men of good family saw smuggling as a safe and entertaining way to make money, and even Sir Robert Walpole, Britain's first Prime Minister, is known to have used an Admiralty barge to run wine up the Thames.

London was by far the largest market for all goods, legal or illegal, and absorbed at least half of all the contraband landed in Britain. Along all the roads to London, depots were established to hold smuggled stocks, and many of the capital's warehouses were exclusively for smuggled and stolen goods – there was even a depot within the Fleet prison. There was a complete trading system running in parallel with legitimate markets, which moved stolen goods and illegal imports.

This alliance of smugglers with thieves and fences helps to dispose of our romantic ideas about the trade. There were many similarities between the smugglers of eighteenth-century England and the bootleggers of Chicago in the 1920s. Each group catered to a very large market, was helped to stay in business by a mixture of bribery, violence and public tolerance, but was fundamentally a criminal conspiracy which would engage in any dirty business to make money. The authorities found that whenever smuggling was suppressed, there was an increase in violent highway robbery as the criminals looked for alternative work. Smugglers transported as convicts were more likely than most other groups of offenders to make a clandestine return to Britain, to hide out among their friends in the underworld networks, and return to a life of crime.

Controlling smuggling

When there were no effective police forces to prevent or detect crime, the conventional English response was to prescribe the highest punishments – usually death – for anyone convicted and hope that each example made would deter others. Perhaps because so many respectable people had a part in it, smuggling did not become a felony until the middle of the eighteenth century, and even then hanging seems only to have been customary where the smugglers had offered armed resistance to the Revenue men.

Old-style commercial smuggling was defeated not by punishment, or even by the improvements in prevention and detection which came after 1816 with the creation of coastguard posts, but by more sensible levels of duty and broader methods of taxation. Once the profits had been cut, the smuggling ended.

A GALLERY OF OLD MURDERERS

For hundreds of years, only the grandest trials were recorded in detail, and we have no more than simple lists of the crimes and investigations, the trials and sentences of ordinary criminals.

By the eighteenth century both the working of the law, with its dependence on precedent, and the appetite of a literate public for lurid stories from the courts, led to a much more careful recording of what was done and said.

Here are four quite different cases, all famous in their day. Each begins with a death, and a charge of murder, but the crimes and their outcomes are very different. To set the scene, let's look at an indictment, the document which brought two men to the dock of the Old Bailey, on trial for their lives.

An indictment for murder

The Jurors[1] for our Lord the King upon their oath present, That Bennet

[1] This was the old Grand Jury, who had to agree that there was a case to answer before a prisoner could be brought to trial.

Allen, late of the parish of St George's Hanover-square, in the county of Middlesex, clerk[2], and Robert Morris, late of the same place, Esq not having the fear of God before their eyes, but being moved and seduced by the instigation of the devil, on the 18th day of June, in the 22nd year of the reign of our Sovereign Lord George the Third, King of Great Britain, &c. with force and arms, at the parish aforesaid, in the county aforesaid, in and upon Lloyd Dulany Esq. in the peace of God and our said Lord the King, then and there being, feloniously, wilfully, and of their malice aforethought[3], did make an assault; and that he, the said Bennet Allen, with a certain pistol, of the value of five shillings[4], then and there charged with gun powder and one leaden bullet, which pistol he, the said Bennet Allen, in his right-hand then and there had and held, then and there feloniously, wilfully, and with malice aforethought, did discharge and shoot off, to, against, and upon him, the said Lloyd Dulany; and that the said Bennet Allen, with the leaden bullet aforesaid, out of the pistol aforesaid, then and there, by force of the gun powder aforesaid, by the said Bennet Allen discharged and shot as aforesaid, then and there, feloniously, wilfully and of his malice aforethought, did strike, penetrate, and wound the said Lloyd Dulany, in and upon the breast of him, the said Lloyd Dulany, below the right pap of the said Lloyd Dulany, giving him the said Lloyd Dulany, then and there, with the leaden bullet aforesaid, so as aforesaid discharged and shot out of the pistol aforesaid, by force of the gun powder aforesaid, by the said Bennet Allen, in and upon the said breast of him the said Lloyd Dulany, below the said right pap of the said Lloyd Dulany, one mortal wound of the depth of three inches, and of the breadth of half an inch, of which said mortal wound he, the said Lloyd Dulany, from the said 18th day of June, in the 22nd year aforesaid, until the 21st day of the said month of June, in the year aforesaid, at the parish aforesaid, in the county aforesaid, did languish, and languishingly did live; on which 21st day of June, in the year aforesaid, the said Lloyd Dulany, at the parish aforesaid, in the county aforesaid, of the mortal wound aforesaid, died: And that the said Robert Morris, at the time of committing the felony and murder aforesaid, then and there, feloniously, wilfully, and of his malice aforethought, was present, aiding, abetting, comforting,

[2] i.e. a clergyman.
[3] For the charge of murder, all these elements had to be present.
[4] The value of the pistol did not matter – here, and throughout the indictment, the jury was simply setting out the evidence it had heard.

assisting, and maintaining the said Bennet Allen, to kill and murder the said Lloyd Dulany, in manner and form aforesaid: And so the indictment charges, That the said Bennet Allen and Robert Morris, then and there, feloniously, wilfully and of their malice aforethought, did kill and murder him, the said Lloyd Dulany, in manner and form aforesaid, against the peace of our said Lord the King, his crown and dignity.

Death in a duel

Personal combat had been used by the courts themselves to decide guilt, but by the eighteenth century duelling had become squalid and worthless. Foolish young men risked death and injury, gambling their lives as readily as they risked their fortunes; bullies used the threat of a duel to humiliate and exploit their victims, and the authorities were eager to stamp out a custom which was often little more than licensed killing.

The charges in the indictment above arose from a duel in Hyde Park in June 1782. Three years before, the Reverend Mr Allen had written an anonymous article which libelled Mr Dulany's brother – the Dulany's were American, and Allen had written that during the rebellion of the American colonies the Dulany family had profited by backing both the king and the rebels.

Lloyd Dulany had tried to find the author of the libel, but Allen waited three years to reveal himself, then wrote a brusque note which amounted to a challenge to a duel. Still a very angry man, Dulany accepted.

The two men met in the evening in Hyde Park – where Allen complained that since he was suffering from a cold, he wanted to move to a drier patch of ground – then at a signal, each man fired a single shot. Dulany fell with a wound to his chest, the bullet having passed through one lung, and died some days later. Allen and his second, the Robert Morris named in the indictment, were charged with murder.

At the trial at the Old Bailey, Allen produced a number of convincing witnesses to his own excellent character, and laid great stress on his own British virtues. Though there was evidence that he had spent some time practising his marksmanship, and that his second had shortened the distance between the two men when they were to fire, Allen declared that his eyesight was very poor, and that the whole incident was no more than an unfortunate mischance.

Mr Justice Buller gave the trial jury very clear direction – if the men met to fight a duel, Allen was guilty of murder: 'Sitting here, it is my duty to tell you what the law is, which I have done in explicit terms; and we must not suffer it to be frittered away by any false or fantastical notions of honour.'

Even so, the jury could not bring itself to convict Allen and Morris of a crime for which they would hang. Morris was acquitted, and Allen's charge reduced to manslaughter: for this he was fined one shilling, and imprisoned for just six months.

Major Strangwayes

John Fussel was a wealthy gentleman, a Dorset landowner who also carried on a business in London. One evening as he sat in his lodgings, at a desk close to the window, a shot was fired: a single shot, but from a gun which had been loaded with three separate bullets – two struck Fussel in the head, the third lodged in the window frame.

Suspicion fell upon Major George Strangwayes. The Major had a sister, a spinster who held a substantial estate that the Major expected to inherit; then Miss Strangwayes announced that she was to marry Fussel. If she married, all her property must pass to her new husband, and the angry Major threatened that he would kill Fussel rather than allow himself to be robbed.

Strangwayes was arrested, but declared himself innocent of the shooting. In those days it was believed that if a murderer touched the body of his victim, fresh blood would flow from the wounds, so Strangwayes was taken from Newgate for the test to be applied. He grasped the hand of the corpse, but of course no blood came forth. The authorities had to try a more practical approach, and took up a suggestion from one of the members of the coroner's jury: a check was made to see if any gunsmith had lent or sold a gun on the day of the murder.

It worked. A man was found who had rented a carbine to Major Strangwayes: he had handed it over just a hundred yards from Fussel's house an hour or so before the murder, and testified that he had loaded it himself – with three bullets. The Major confessed at once.

Strangwayes was not tried, nor was he hanged. When his case came to court, he refused to enter a plea, and refused to tell the court who had fired the fatal shot. In such cases our courts now enter a plea of Not

Guilty on behalf of the accused, and proceed to a trial, but Strangways knew that by refusing to plead he prevented any trial or conviction. In those days the Crown seized the property of anyone convicted of a felony, and by avoiding conviction, the Major made sure that his estate was safe.

The price of this choice was a terrible death. The penalty for refusing to plead was to be pressed under heavy weights – a process known as *peine forte et dure* – until either a plea was forthcoming or the accused was killed. On 28 February 1654 Major Strangwayes was laid out in a

This was the fate of Major Strangwayes: spreadeagled in the Press Yard of Newgate prison. Those who refused to plead were crushed to death beneath intolerable weights.

long mourning cloak on a floor in Newgate, a board placed on his chest, and within minutes he was crushed by the great weight placed over his heart.

Elizabeth Brownrigg

It took a great deal to shock Londoners in the eighteenth century: they were used to squalor of a depth that we cannot imagine, and accustomed to death in almost all its forms, from disease to cold-blooded killing.

The cruelty of Elizabeth Brownrigg made her notorious. This was a portrait of her as a prisoner, and the artist has tried to display her hypocrisy – though she holds a prayer book or Bible, her face is set in a disagreeable frown.

Even so, the crimes of Elizabeth Brownrigg were vile enough to shock and enrage even the most hardened. In the 1760s Mrs Brownrigg was a midwife, who had been given permission to open a lying-in hospital, and hired young girls to assist in household duties. At first she treated them well, but in a transformation which we shall never understand,

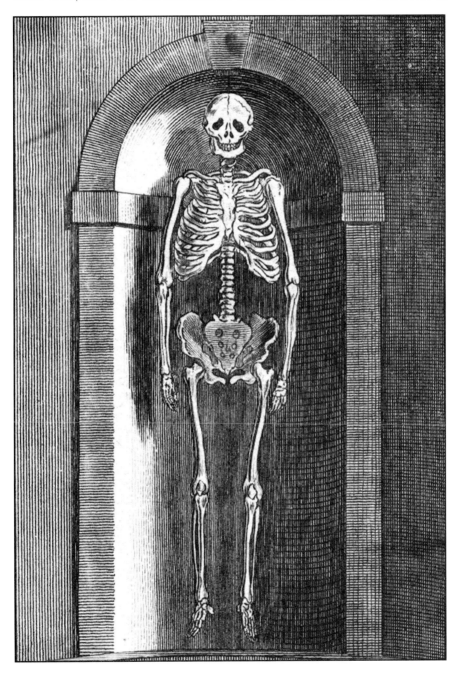

THE SKELETON OF
ELIZABETH
BROWNRIGG
So despised was Mrs Brownrigg that not only was her body sent to the anatomists, but her bones remained on view at Surgeons' Hall for generations.

she became a brutal and cruel tyrant who repeatedly attacked and neglected her helpers.

Details were later to emerge of ways in which three of the girls had been abused. For the slightest error she stripped and flogged them, chained and starved and imprisoned them; when she had no more strength to whip them, they were subjected to freezing cold. When it seemed they might confide in one of the residents, Mrs Brownrigg tried to cut out their tongues with scissors. Stories of the girls' plight spread, and when parish authorities called, they were allowed to take one girl. Insisting on looking further, they found one of the girls locked in a cupboard, weak from starvation.

Mr Brownrigg was seized and a warrant issued for the arrest of Brownrigg and her son, who had fled in disguise. By the time the case came to trial one girl had died of her mistreatment and although her son and husband were sent to prison, Mrs Brownrigg was sentenced to hang. There was intense public curiosity about the case, and outrage at the outward piety and raw sadism which seemed to combine in the prisoner's character. She went to Tyburn to her death through vast and hate-filled crowds, and her dissected body was put on show at Surgeons' Hall to ensure that 'the heinousness of her cruelty might make the more lasting impression in the minds of the spectators.'

Catherine Hayes

On 2 March 1725 a wooden pole, taller than a man, was erected in the yard of St Margaret's church in Westminster. On the top, a human head, freshly washed and with its hair neatly combed, had been impaled for display.

The thousands who joined the curious staring crowd soon learned that this was an attempt by the authorities to discover the identity of the man, whose head had been found in a bucket in the Thames mud near the Horse Ferry. Some spectators thought they recognised a coal merchant called Hayes, but when they asked at his home, they were told that though Hayes was away, he was alive and well. Some days passed, and the magistrates gave instructions for the head to be preserved; a woman from the East End became convinced that the head was that of her missing husband, and a fresh search was made for the rest of the body.

Three friends of Mr Hayes, fobbed off by Mrs Hayes with an unlikely story, went at last to the authorities. Mrs Hayes, a man called Billings, who may well have been her son by an earlier liaison, and a woman called Mrs Springate were all arrested. Confronted with the head of her husband, preserved in a jar, Mrs Hayes put on an affecting show of horrified surprise and grief: she wept as she clutched the jar, asked for the head to be pulled out so that she might kiss it several times, and asked for a lock of the hair as a keepsake.

The magistrates were unimpressed, and evidence of her guilt soon began to mount. Hayes' body was discovered in a ditch in Marylebone,

A grisly but effective way to identify a victim – Catherine Hayes was captured because her husband's head was identified as it stood upon a pole in Westminster.

and a lodger called Wood who had lived with the family was captured. When questioned, Wood told a long story of how he and Billings had been drawn by Mrs Hayes into a plot to get Hayes drunk and kill him for his money. The two men had killed Hayes with a hatchet and then at her suggestion the head had been cut off the corpse to prevent identification. In turn Billings, too, confessed and the quite innocent Mrs Springate was released.

Catherine Hayes first protested her total innocence, but when convicted she admitted that she had been part of the conspiracy, but argued that she had not struck the fatal blow. What Mrs Hayes dreaded was the punishment prescribed for women who killed their husbands – burning at the stake.

To kill a husband was legally regarded as petty treason, when burning was regarded as a more decent death for women traitors than the hanging, drawing and quartering laid down for men. The court decided that no exception would be made in the case of Mrs Hayes, and she would go to the stake.

As she awaited execution, Mrs Hayes tried to kill herself with poison, but her attempt was discovered, and on 9 May 1726 she was drawn on a sledge – again part of the ritual for traitors – to Tyburn. Wood had already died of gaol fever, but Billings was taken on the same day and hanged, as Mrs Hayes was chained to a stake near the gallows.

It was the custom at a burning for the hangman (often with a bribe to encourage him) to tighten a cord around the victim's neck and ensure a quick death, but on this occasion the flames rose too quickly, the executioner's hand was burned, and he let go of the cord. The Tyburn mob, usually so callous, was horrified to see Catherine Hayes burn slowly to death, pushing at the piles of wood and crying out in pain.

The bizarre brutality of the murder, the investigation, and the execution made the case notorious: during the Victorian fashion for novels based on historic true crimes Thackeray published a fictional account called *Catherine*.

THE FORGERS

What one man can make, another can fake; forgery is one of the great criminal professions. The cash in our pockets may now be well protected by intricate printing and elaborate watermarks, but the brake linings in our cars and the watches on our wrists may be counterfeits. Some crooks take wealth, others make it.

Forgery means, very simply, making any false object or document to defraud or deceive. In early times, it was often the seal on a document which proved it genuine, because even those who could not read or write would recognise the crest or design on the seal. A servant who stole or copied a seal could misuse all his master's authority: it was rather like stealing a credit card which gave not only cash but every kind of power and privilege. This was such a breach of trust that in 1176 forgery by a servant became a variety of treason, for which men would be punished by hanging, drawing and quartering, and women by burning at the stake.

Since there was no paper money, and most people neither owned nor used any documents at all, it took several hundred years for forgery in general to become a crime, but by Tudor times the combination of religious struggles and a vast increase in trade made false documents much more dangerous. In Elizabeth I's reign an Act dismissed as 'small, mild and easy' past punishments for forgery, and prescribed that a forger could be put in the pillory, have his ears cut off, his nostrils slit, and lose his hand. As if these weren't enough, all his property was forfeit, and he would suffer perpetual imprisonments. The final, almost inevitable step came when forgery became a felony under King Charles I: forgers were now to be hanged.

When the law turned against forgery, it was because papers – and false papers – had come to carry great weight. The old rich had kept their wealth as land, and although the occasional scandal arose when a deed was forged, it was a crime which affected only a single victim. The growth of a huge trading empire made the merchants and their investors rich, and their wealth depended much more on documents. Valuable cargoes, and the money to pay for them, were handed over because the paperwork looked right.

IMITATION BANKNOTE
George Cruikshank, the caricaturist, was outraged by the law which demanded death for forgery – classed as a treason, and punished by hanging for men, burning for women. In 1818 he taunted the authorities with this, his own grisly counterfeit of a banknote.

The greatest opportunities came with the use of paper money: the Bank of England was founded in 1694, and soon produced its first rather crude 'Accountable Notes', but it was only a fortnight before the first forged £100 note was discovered! For this crime four men were fined and pilloried, but the dangers were so plain that in 1697 banknote forgery was made punishable by death.

The notes themselves were simple by the standards of today, and to copy them was still a matter of manual skill. A man called Mathison drew attention to himself in the 1770s by his frequent visits to the bank: it seemed odd to the clerks that on each occasion he either drew or deposited a single £20 note. Mathison's method seems very laborious – each time he withdrew a note, he took it home, copied it by hand, passed his new copy, then waited some time before returning the original note to the bank. For his meticulous work, Mathison was gaining no more than he might have earned in a couple of months in a legitimate trade, and at much greater risk – he was of course hanged.

There were many banks, each issuing its own currency, and even though cheques as we know them came much later, money changed hands in a hundred different ways: certificates of every kind promised on paper that they were worth hard cash. This was a system that depended utterly on the trustworthiness of the person offering the paper, and was wide open to forgery by the criminal and the desperate. With no effective means of preventing or investigating forgery, the law depended on the deterrent effect of the death sentence.

It is said that the Bank of England is still haunted by the ghost of Sarah Whitehead, who went mad when her brother Philip, who had worked there, was sent to the gallows in 1811 for forging cheques. After the hanging she returned each day to the Bank for twenty-five years, pitifully looking for her brother. When she died, she was buried in the churchyard within the Bank – now a garden – and it is here that her figure has been seen.

Year after year forgers were sentenced to death, and when we look at the fates of convicts it is startling to find that although many murderers, burglars and robbers had their sentences reduced to transportation or imprisonment, forgers very rarely escaped death. Despite this, many criminal gangs included coining among their activities, hiding their apparatus for melting down and casting deep inside the rookeries where the watchmen could not penetrate. Most commonly, they amassed clippings – small chips of metal from the edges of other coins, removing just enough to leave an acceptable coin – or melted down stolen coins to produce metal which could be turned into coins of higher value. From their dens they would pass out their products to a network of pickpockets, prostitutes and innkeepers to put the coins into circulation.

Forgery of the king's currency was a treason, and although the punishment for men was reduced in practice from hanging, drawing and quartering to simple hanging, women were still burned at the stake. Burning seems to have had a particular sinister appeal for the mob, perhaps as a novelty among the hangings, perhaps because it had associations with witches and wickedness. When Barbara Spencer, burned for coining in 1721, was tied to the stake she protested at 'the dirt and stones thrown by the mob behind her, which prevented her from thinking sedately on futurity.'

Burnings drew unusually large crowds: twenty thousand went to Tyburn to watch Phoebe Harris go to the stake for coining in 1786. Executions were moved to Newgate soon after, and the very last woman to be burned perished there. She was Christian Murphy, who had been convicted with her husband of forging coin, and after he had joined seven others on the gallows on 18 March 1789, Mrs Murphy was led to a small gibbet, strung up, and then covered with bundles of wood to be burned.

Although they appealed to the crowds, these executions inevitably made many victims reluctant to report a crime – they wanted restitution, but not to cost a man his life – and juries must have been more than usually inclined to acquit against the evidence if they felt any sympathy for the prisoner. The very last of the hundreds of executions for forgery took place in 1829, and the law was changed to reduce the penalty to a maximum of life imprisonment three years later.

Doctor Dodd

The most famous victim of the law's savage punishment of forgers was Doctor William Dodd, a preacher whose eloquence caught the fancy of fashionable society, and promoted him from an East End curacy to appointment as a Royal Chaplain. His appetite for good living grew even faster than his popularity, and when his debts threatened to overwhelm him he was caught trying to bribe his way into a more profitable parish.

Dismissed by the king as a chaplain, and pursued by his creditors, Dodd sold his chapel and took the fatally foolish step of forging the signature of the Earl of Chesterfield to a bond worth £4200. He was not attempting to steal from Chesterfield, but to use the bond as security for a loan, and the deception was quickly discovered by a sharp-eyed lawyer.

It still seemed possible for Dodd to save himself. He offered to return the money he had raised, his offer was accepted, and with the help of friends Dodd gave back £3900, but still he was sent for trial and convicted. There was strong public protest from those who thought it wrong to prosecute when his repayments had been accepted: Dr Johnson had assisted Dodd in preparing his defence, there was a strong recommendation for mercy at his trail, and a petition bearing 23,000 names called for his life to be spared. Appeals to the Lord Chief Justice, the Privy Council, and the King all failed, and Dodd went to Tyburn in 1777.

THE GARROTTERS

As every Sherlock Holmes film reminds us, Victorian London was foggy and ill-lit, every sound muffled by the soot and sulphur that hung in the air. The New Police had made the main streets of London much safer, but away from the few lit thoroughfares, down the alleyways and backstreets, thieves still waited to snatch from the unwary, or to strike them down if they resisted. In the 1850s a new terror stalked the streets – the garrotter.

It was the technique of garrotting that was so alarming: instead of snatching and running, or threatening the victim until he handed over his valuables, garrotters moved straight to violence – without warning, the victim would find rope, a cloth, or a strong arm around his throat as he was strangled from behind, the grip tightening until he could neither shout nor breathe. Then other hands would roughly turn out his pockets and seize his belongings, before he was thrown to the ground gasping for air, perhaps kicked a couple of times to stop him raising the alarm.

This was a method as old as robbery itself, but it seems that the quick success of just one gang gave robbers a new and effective technique for the policed streets of London. It was marvellously quick, the gang could be sure of grabbing whatever the victim was carrying without a struggle, and leave him unable to give chase or call for help.

Garrotters became bolder, came out of the alleyways into the broad main streets, among daytime crowds. They no longer waited for a stray passer-by, but systematically pursued anyone who might be carrying the takings of a business, and struck into the most prosperous and respectable neighbourhoods – they robbed an MP between Parliament and his club, and none of the five constables on patrol in the area saw or heard a thing.

Among the many victims were a very few who died, throats crushed by unskilled robbers, or perhaps because the garrotting method was being used in many ordinary fights and attacks.

Newspapers seized on this new terror, called every street robbery a garrotting, and encouraged public panic. This probably helped the technique to spread to the provinces, and reports from out of town in turn increased the fear in London. Anti-garrotting societies were formed, and armed citizens went on patrol to defeat the menace, attacking and seizing anyone suspicious – usually quite innocent men, sometimes anti-garrotters themselves. In the face of the vast outcry, courts and Parliament were both driven to excesses. When the panic was at its height in 1863 more criminals hanged than for a generation – the courts were more ready to condemn, and the authorities less willing to commute sentences – and Parliament passed the Garrotting Act, which added flogging to the usual lengthy prison sentences. Not only were the convicts to receive great numbers of lashes, but the punishment would be inflicted in instalments – between the floggings time was allowed for recuperation, and for the dread of the next whipping to grow.

GARROTTING

It seemed that a new crime had crept from the slums to strike down respectable Londoners, a threat spreading even into their new suburbs. With enormous relish the Victorian Press reported the menace of the lurking, short-necked thug.

Garrotting did decline very rapidly, and to the public this was proof that flogging prevented violent crime. In fact, it now seems more likely that the determined street robbers were few, and that many of the reported robberies had been minor copy-cat crimes: once the few dozens of early garrotters had been caught, police were able to develop their networks of informants to catch their successors. Newspapers lost interest, and garrotting had had its day.

THE SWINDLERS

> *As a city of traders and the centre of banking, London has always drawn poor men hoping to be rich, and rich men hoping to be richer. Ready to greet them and empty their pockets is an army of fraudsters, con men and manipulators.*

From the earliest times, a man might be cheated on the simplest purchase; if he came to town to buy a horse, he was likely to leave with an animal much older and much feebler than he knew. The traders of West Smithfield were as cunning as their motor trade descendants: knowing that some colours of horse were more popular, they would respray their animals; to give a horse the black marks on its teeth common in younger beasts, they applied a branding iron; to make a horse appear lively they would beat it until the bruises were sensitive to the rider's gentlest touch. It is astonishing how many motor trade tricks had their counterparts – just as a modern rogue slaps filler onto bodywork rust or damage, a dishonest horse dealer slapped mud onto injuries and the signs of disease.

On a larger scale, markets in commodities such as corn and fish were manipulated just as energetically and unscrupulously as stocks and shares may be in our own time. Most intriguing of all was a new criminal class – the projectors – which took advantage of the Elizabethan explosion of exploration and manufacture. Those who had been brave enough to invest at the right time had made quick fortunes from the exploitation of the Indies, and the public was eager to find the next great opportunity for profit. The projectors offered them, according to Jonson, a chance to get in on the ground floor of schemes to dress the skins of dogs, to make wine from raisins, and to reclaim all the submerged land in England.

Even these oddities were to be eclipsed during the insanity of the South Sea Bubble. In 1720 the South Sea Company issued a grandiose proposal to take over the National Debt, in return for payments and trading privileges. The idea found favour: Parliament was quick to approve, the Company's stock soared, and investment fever seized a gullible public. There were eager subscribers for every lunatic venture, from the foolish to the utterly bogus, from a million-pound project for a perpetual motion machine to the notorious 'undertaking of great advantage, but nobody to know what it is.'

Within months the bubble had burst. Though the South Sea proposal was not in itself fraudulent, it had been propelled through Parliament by bribery, and the stock price had been jacked up by 'very artificial engines and secret springs'. When the manoeuvres of the Company were exposed, the entire market in speculative stocks collapsed. South Sea investors received some compensation out of the estates confiscated from directors, but they were the fortunate ones.

With every expansion of trade the opportunities for fraud increased, and there was no easier or more profitable way to exploit the growing market than to operate from within the largely unregulated banks and finance houses. At the beginning of the nineteenth century, scandal followed scandal as a succession of bankers were exposed: Fauntleroy, executed in 1824 for forging powers of attorney; Stephenson, the bank partner and MP who fled the country with £70,000 of depositors' money; Sadleir, who stole at least £400,000, then sat on Hampstead Heath to drink prussic acid from a small silver cream jug; Pullinger, who was only a cashier but stole £263,000 using false pass-books.

Every legitimate feature of the grand Victorian expansion, each genuine invention or profitable new industry seemed to have its criminal counterpart – there were fraudulent railway share issues, fraudulent docks, and even the construction of the Panama Canal was fraudulently financed. Some criminals were men who had started honestly enough, then became enmeshed in their own underhand dealings, but there were also flamboyant rogues who lived by raw and brazen cheating, outrageous showmen like Horatio Bottomley.

Bottomley's principal skill was in exploiting the new mass market for newspapers and magazines which had been created in the late Victorian years by improved education and cheaper production. In the 1880s he founded a local paper called the *Hackney Hansard*, which could have been a legitimate success, but Bottomley used it as the foundation for his first elaborate fraud. He sold thousands of shares in a scheme which would merge printing and publishing houses in England and Austria, but most of the money went straight into his own pocket; at his trial he used the eloquence which had sold the shares to obtain a triumphant acquittal.

Time and again he floated companies, declared high dividends to boost the share price, then sold his own holding and abandoned the failing firm. When angry shareholders pursued him, he charmed them into buying stock in another great venture; when sued or prosecuted he used a broad knowledge of the law, all his powers of persuasion – and timely bribes to opposition witnesses – to walk away free.

In 1906 Bottomley founded *John Bull*, a successful weekly magazine which not only yielded legitimate profits, but ran advertisements for all his shady companies. There was even a third way of turning a profit: Bottomley threatened to publish damaging articles about companies which did not pay him off.

He was elected as a Liberal MP in 1905, and although he was forced to resign his seat in 1912 – by a financial scandal, of course – he kept his political ambitions alive. When war came, he saw the profit in patriotism, and stormed about the country to make recruiting speeches

HORATIO BOTTOMLEY
A tubthumping self-publicist and a persuasive defendant in court, Horatio Bottomley exploited jingoism to become a prince among fraudsters. This cartoon of 1918 mocked him, but he was then in the midst of a last great swindle.

while *John Bull* trumpeted crude Hun-hating jingoism. As 'the friend of the little man' Bottomley was re-elected to Parliament as an Independent, and for the poor who could not afford to buy the Victory Bonds issued by the Government when the war was won, he created the Victory Bond Club.

The Club was his last great swindle. To pay for his champagne, his young mistresses, his horses and his homes, Bottomley had stolen £150,000 from the funds, and even his great courtroom skills could not save him from a prison sentence. When he came out of gaol, none of his old schemes and manoeuvres would work, and he died in poverty.

One last fraudster deserves a place in this history of swindling, as a rare example of the kind of crook normally found only in novels – the perfectly respectable expert who sees a way to turn his legitimate profession into a source of criminal profit. His name was Harris, and he was an expert on fires.

Fire-raising may be a demented act, part of a large riot or disorder, or a desperate attempt by a failing businessman to restore his fortunes with the insurance money, but in the 1930s a vast and complex arson racket was exposed which had yielded hundreds of thousands of pounds each year. The partners in this conspiracy were not shady underworld figures, but insurance assessors, accountants, even firemen, all led and controlled by a well-known and reputable fire assessor called Leopold Harris.

Harris's method had been to finance a large number of agents, each of whom set up in a business which needed very flammable stocks and materials. When insurance cover had been arranged, and a few premiums paid, the premises would be set alight, and a claim submitted. The size and value of the stocks would be exaggerated, all evidence of deliberate arson suppressed by the conspirators, and the profit safely divided.

It took two years of thorough and conscientious investigation to produce evidence on twenty-nine major fires, and sixteen of the plotters were convicted at the Old Bailey in 1933. As the ringleader, Harris was sentenced to fifteen years in prison, a very long sentence indeed for the time, but Harris' knowledge and expertise were so valuable that he spent the early years of his sentence as a case consultant to the authorities and insurance companies: it is said that his cell at Maidstone prison became an overstuffed office full of dossiers on which he worked every day.

JACK THE RIPPER

Within less than fifty days, within one square mile in the grimmest streets of the East End, five women were slaughtered. The killer was never captured, and we shall probably never know his true name, but he is infamous as Jack the Ripper.

Even in the briefest outline the facts are chilling. The first victim was found on 31 August 1888: Mary Anne Nicholls, aged forty-two, was found in Buck's Row with her throat cut. Just a week later forty-seven-year-old Annie Chapman was murdered in the same way, and disembowelled, half a mile away. Then on 30 September two women – Elizabeth Stride, aged forty-five, and Catherine Eddowes, aged forty-three – were murdered in less than an hour; finally on 9 November Mary Kelly, only twenty-five years old, was killed in her room. All five women were prostitutes, all had been appallingly mutilated in ways which seemed to suggest that the killer had surgical knowledge and skill. After the final murder, behind closed doors and with no fear of interruption, Mary Kelly's heart and kidneys had been removed and laid out on her table.

The title 'Jack the Ripper' was not a newspaper invention. It was the name used by a man claiming to be the killer in letters received by the press and the police between the second and third murders. Every major crime attracts false confessions, but one letter announced that he would 'clip the lady's ears', and post-mortems on Eddowes and Stride both revealed attempts to remove their ears. In the absence of other evidence the letters were taken very seriously, though the author was never identified.

Though East Enders were used to casual violence, the methodical savagery of the attacks caused a panic of fear and revulsion, redoubling with each discovery. Citizen's Vigilance Committees were formed, and civilians stalked through the streets and alleyways to join the police patrols which were tripled after the first two murders. Six hundred police officers were eventually drafted into the area, but Jack was neither deterred nor captured, and became an ever more terrifying figure – he was more than a crude beast, he was a subtle and cunning planner who could weave through any cordon to kill at pleasure then slip back into the shadows and disappear.

Every new murder was a humiliation to the hapless police, whose failure to catch Jack aroused fury and contempt in the streets, in the press, and in Parliament. A constable passed the spot where Eddowes was killed at half past one in the morning, and returned only fifteen minutes later to find her disembowelled body. Sir Charles Warren, the Commissioner of the Metropolitan Police, was everywhere criticised for his plodding conduct of the investigation, and he resigned after the murder of Mary Kelly. Everyone had an opinion – if only this had been done ... if these measures had only been taken earlier ... wasn't it obvious that....

The whole story is a mystery; there are many people who believe that Jack committed more than these five killings, but cannot easily agree on just which deaths should be added to the list. All the Victorian amateur detectives who gave Scotland Yard free advice have been followed by generations of investigators who have tried without success to identify the killer. In hundreds of books every piece of evidence has been examined in minute detail, every lead pursued.

Let's review some of the suspects against whom cases have been assembled. They could almost be called the Gentlemen and the Players – rather as some people find it difficult to believe that a commoner like Shakespeare could have written so well, and cast about for a noble substitute, the socially conscious sleuths have always wanted Jack to be high-born, a notable, even a Royal.

Those who like snobbery with violence have often put forward the name of the Duke of Clarence, Queen Victoria's grandson and a man with a great appetite for the low life. Gossip at the time suggested that a member of the royal family was involved, and some have thought Clarence did the murders himself, but he was at Sandringham at the time of the last murder. Others wondered whether his tutor – James Kenneth Stephen, the uncle of Virginia Woolf – was the killer, but evidence that compared Stephen's poetry with letters received by the police has never been convincing.

The most elaborate tale was that Clarence married in secret a Catholic girl who bore him a son, and that Mary Kelly was nurse to the boy. When she plotted with other prostitutes to extort money from the Duke, Clarence commissioned the Queen's physician, Sir William Gull, to hunt down and kill every member of the blackmail conspiracy: Gull in turn was protected by a number of highly placed fellow Freemasons.

THE FIFTH VICTIM OF THE WHITECHAPEL FIEND.

FINDING THE MUTILATED BODY IN MITRE SQARE.

Front page news – all Jack the Ripper's murders, and the confused helplessness of the police, were relished in the Victorian picture papers.

The intricacy of this version appealed to many people, but its origins lie in a deliberate hoax, and it has been established that Gull suffered an incapacitating stroke well before the murders.

A second category of candidate may seem more promising. Two other men are known to have killed several women each in London at much the same time that Jack was on the loose.

The first of these was the favourite suspect of Chief Inspector Abberline, who had directed the investigation. He was a Pole called Severin Klowssoski who had taken the name of George Chapman. He lived in Whitechapel, practised as a 'barber-surgeon', and his mistress told the police that he frequently returned home in the early hours of the morning. Though he fitted the description given of a man seen with Mary Kelly, no further evidence could be found, and it may be no more than coincidence that thirteen years later Chapman was arrested for the murder of his wife by antimony poisoning. This was not his only killing: when the bodies of two past partners – a previous wife and a mistress – were exhumed, they too were discovered to have been poisoned, and Chapman was hanged for these crimes in 1903.

Nonetheless Chapman becomes an unlikely Jack when we consider that he chose a very different method of killing his victims, and relied on their deaths being overlooked as natural; further, he killed close companions not working prostitutes – he was already a bigamist before he killed, and his motive seems to have been cold-blooded personal convenience rather than a vast rage against all womankind.

A second serial killer of women has sometimes been promoted as a possible Jack. Neill Cream was the convicted sadistic murderer of four prostitutes, and he was a doctor. His last words as the trapdoor of the Newgate gallows opened under his feet were 'I am Jack the …'. But Cream's viciousness lay in persuading women to take strychnine and die painful deaths, and at the time of the Whitechapel murders he was serving a sentence in the Joliet Penitentiary in Chicago for another poisoning.

A number of investigations have tried to identify Jack by concentrating on one of the major puzzles of the case: why did Jack stop so suddenly? Why only five victims (or just possibly six, if an earlier killing which involved no mutilation is included)? If some unholy urge had driven him to kill so frequently in such a short time, what can have prevented a sixth, seventh, or eighth atrocity?

One answer may be that he did not stop of his own will, but that he died, or was imprisoned, or confined to a mental hospital. This logic led the police to suspect very strongly a barrister called Druitt who threw himself into the Thames at the beginning of December 1888. But there seems never to have been any other stronger evidence to link Druitt closely to the murders, while there were other clear reasons for his depression and suicide.

A final candidate for our shortlist was identified by General William Booth, the founder of the Salvation Army. He was convinced that his own secretary was the killer, because the man seemed to foretell the killing of another woman a couple of years after the Jack killings, then disappeared. No one else seems ever to have shared Booth's opinion.

At a conference held by the Police History Society to mark the one hundredth anniversary of that autumn of bloodletting, police officers, criminologists, and students of the case were invited, once and for all, to select the most likely name from a list of ten principal suspects. There was no useful consensus; Jack has disappeared into the fog for ever.

THE SIEGE OF SIDNEY STREET

It is still uncommon for the police or the criminals of the capital to carry guns, but on one extraordinary morning – 3 January 1911 – the greatest peacetime battle in English history brought armed police and troops onto the streets of London.

In late December 1910 three police officers had been shot dead and two others wounded when they interrupted a group of armed men preparing to burgle a jeweller's shop. There was intense public outrage, and the police were utterly determined to track down the killers and avenge the deaths. They discovered that the killers were members of a Russian anarchist group led by Peter Piatkow – 'Peter the Painter' – and within days succeeded in tracking down two of the gang to a house in Sidney Street in the East End.

Both the Metropolitan and City police provided men for a force of four hundred men which surrounded the terrorists' hideout and stealthily evacuated their neighbours in the early hours of the morning. A strong cordon was thrown around the building, including officers armed with rifles, shotguns and revolvers, then at first light the anarchists were awakened and called on to surrender. They replied with shots, a police sergeant fell wounded, and from then on each side kept up steady fire.

After a few hours, military help was requested, and permission to bring in the troops was given by the Liberal Home Secretary, Winston Churchill. A detachment of Scots Guards arrived from the Tower of London garrison to join in the shooting, and at midday Churchill himself came to observe the operation.

He found an extraordinary scene, with spectators milling in the streets, and perched among the armed police in and on buildings all around, paying up to ten shillings for a good rooftop seat; a postman

Police armed with sporting shotguns mustered to join in the siege of Sidney Street. As the morning wore on, they were joined by troops with rifles, and when the Home Secretary – Winston Churchill – arrived, he was even to call for artillery.

had even sauntered through the cordon earlier to deliver letters to the house next door to the anarchists. During the morning several bystanders had been hit by ricochets, and still wanting vengeance the police were urging that the house be stormed. Churchill agreed that artillery should be brought from St John's Wood to demolish the house before the police and troops moved in.

Then quite suddenly the house caught fire, and the terrorists found themselves trapped between the flames and the shots of the besiegers. Eventually the roof collapsed and several firemen were injured trying to extinguish the fire. When the remains of the house were explored, the bodies of two men were uncovered; neither of them was Peter the Painter – he was never found.

Though they may have enjoyed the excitement, Londoners soon decided that the seven hours of siege had been a shambles. They thought the use of troops was absurdly excessive, and felt that Churchill had indulged his own appetite for excitement but made management of the incident more difficult. Though they admired the courage and determination of the police, they loathed the use of so many firearms: the indiscipline of the siege strengthened many people's belief that law enforcement should not require guns.

THE MASTER CRIMINAL

If ever there was a real-life Professor Moriarty, a true Napoleon of Crime, he was Doctor Talbot Bridgewater, whose medical practice in Oxford Street was the front for a forgery factory, and a headquarters in which every variety of criminal enterprise was carefully planned, from burglaries to bank robberies.

At the time of his arrest in 1905 Doctor Bridgewater was a successful legitimate medical man with what was described as a 'tremendous medical practice', living in a mansion in Sussex and accepted locally as being quite respectable, if rather inclined to put on the air of a country squire. In London he kept rather coarser company, recruiting men with names like Dicer Cobb, Bill the Barman, and The Key King, and giving them paid employment as assistants in the practice as cover for their real work.

Bridgewater's operation did not mass-produce banknotes or coin. His specialism was the use of stolen cheques and certificates, usually altered to increase their value enormously, and his workforce included thieves to steal the papers, craftsmen forgers to improve them, and men who would present the cheques without drawing suspicion.

When only the prosperous had bank accounts and drew cheques upon them, banks took few precautions against forgery, and relied on little more than the eyesight, common sense and instincts of their cashiers. This was enough to stop the occasional crude alteration by a nervous amateur, but left them and their clients vulnerable to systematic plunder by a professional gang.

Bridgewater's men stole cheques and money orders of all kinds, burgling houses and opening pillar boxes to get their hands on the raw material. Then, before the thefts had been reported, the gang would choose the most promising papers, ripe for alteration and drawn on substantial accounts. The forgers would use acids and bleaches to remove any 'crossing' – the pen strokes across the cheques which would prevent payment across the counter – and a range of inks and nibs to increase the value of the cheque and make any other necessary alterations. If the changes were still too visible, the cheque would be folded or crumpled to obscure them. Finally a respectably dressed, well-spoken member of the team would then hurry to the issuing bank to turn the cheque into cash.

In this way a secure cheque made out for £9 might be turned into an open cheque for £98. This reassuringly odd amount was moderate enough not to arouse suspicion or require the manager to make enquiries with his client. Any ordinary checking would of course show the bank that the signature itself was authentic. Bridgewater's men had no need to be greedy in any one transaction: their safety and their substantial profit lay in achieving a steady turnover of tens and hundreds rather than thousands of pounds.

It was soon obvious to the banks and the police that this flow of high-quality forgeries must come from a single clever source, but for years they made little progress in tracking down the gang. The greatest risk to any large operation comes when a crook is captured, and is offered a deal to betray his fellows, but when Bill the Barman was sent to prison he hanged himself, and as the police came to arrest him, Dicer blew his brains out.

It was probably to keep his secrets safe that Bridgewater made his most public mistake. Criminal gossip had already linked the doctor's name with a forgery operation when he took the foolhardy step of entering the witness box at the Old Bailey to give an alibi for one of his employees. He swore that the man in the dock, charged with attempting to pass a forged cheque, was nowhere near a bank at the time, but working at his dispenser at the Oxford Street consulting rooms. This bold perjury helped his man to go free, but proved to the police that Bridgewater was up to no good, and they started to take a very close interest in the doctor.

It was The Key King who finally told all. His name was Robert Fisher, and he was much the cleverest of the Oxford Street crew. He had invented a patent lock which was installed by several London banks – though, curiously, he never used his knowledge of the lock to rob them. He was a forger, a burglar, and pillar-box 'buster'. Caught and sentenced to ten years in prison, Fisher believed that the doctor had cheated him of some proceeds, and told all he knew about the operation.

Warrants were issued, and when the police went to Oxford Street to call on Bridgewater, they found an extraordinary criminal enterprise hiding behind the respectability of the practice. There were three sets of rooms, linked by elaborate systems of telephones and signal bells, stocked with the tools of forgery and burglary, and staffed by several well-known crooks. Bridgewater blustered, proclaimed his trial 'an outrage of justice', but was convicted on a single charge and sent to prison for seven years. By a strange coincidence, while he was serving his time another doctor, also a tenant at 59 Oxford Street, achieved even greater notoriety – his name was Crippen.

A GALLERY OF MODERN MURDERERS

Doctor Crippen

The last great criminal sensation in England before the First World War was the capture, trial and execution of Dr Hawley Harvey Crippen, who had poisoned his wife then dismembered her.

Doctor Crippen was a small man of meek appearance, an American from Michigan who came to London in 1900 with his large flamboyant second wife Cora, a brash woman who had pursued an unsuccessful singing career under the name of Belle Elmore. Though he had studied medicine, Crippen worked in Oxford Street as a manager for a patent medicine company, and it was at his office, during 1907, that he fell in love with a demure, attractive typist called Ethel le Neve.

A camera was smuggled into Bow Street Court to capture this photograph of Dr Crippen and his mistress Ethel le Neve as they stood in the dock.

During January 1910 Doctor Crippen ordered some hyposcine, a vegetable poison used in small doses for the treatment of mental patients; at the end of that month Mrs Crippen disappeared from view. Her husband was to tell friends that she had gone back to America, and then that she had died, but on 12 March Miss le Neve moved into the Crippen house. Among those who knew the couple, concern grew into suspicion, and at the end of June the police were notified.

On 8 July two police officers interviewed Crippen at home, and this time he said that all his previous accounts of his wife's departure had been lies, and that in fact she had gone to Chicago with a lover. The police then circulated a description of Mrs Crippen, but when they returned a few days later, the doctor had disappeared from both his office and his home. The house was searched thoroughly and some remains of Cora Crippen were discovered buried beneath the cellar floor. The body had been expertly dissected to remove flesh from bone, and the head, limbs and skeleton were never found.

By the time a warrant could be issued, Crippen and le Neve were aboard the SS *Montrose* bound for Canada, he travelling as Mr Robinson and le Neve in boys clothes as his son. The master of the *Montrose*, Captain Kendall, had received a description of the fugitives and when he saw odd signs of affection between the Robinsons he sent a message to the police by wireless telegraph. Two police officers were able to take a fast ship out of Liverpool which overtook the *Montrose*, and arrested the lovers in Quebec. This was the very first time that the newly invented radio had been used in a criminal case.

Brought back to trial, Crippen did little to defend himself but insisted that le Neve, charged as his accessory, had known nothing of the murder. He was convicted, and hanged on 23 November 1910; Le Neve was acquitted, and survived until the 1960s.

Edith Thompson and Frederick Bywaters

On 3 October 1922 Edith and Percy Thompson spent the evening at the Criterion Theatre, watching a farce called *The Dippers*. As they walked to their home in Ilford a young man rushed from the shadows and stabbed Mr Thompson. Mrs Thompson cried for someone to help her husband, but he was dying.

Next day she named the attacker – it was her lover, a man eight years younger than herself called Frederick Bywaters, who had recently returned from a year overseas, a year in which he and Mrs Thompson had exchanged vivid letters. Though she had taken no part in planning the fatal attack, Edith Thompson joined Bywaters in the dock at the Old Bailey, accused of inciting him to kill. The court heard a pathetic story of suburban passion. She was a twenty-eight-year-old manageress, he was a clerk eight years younger. Her letters revealed that she had made inept attempts to poison her husband, but that her feelings were hopelessly immature:

> 'Yes, darlint you are jealous of him,' she wrote '– but I want you to be – he has the right by law, to all that you have the right to by nature and love – yes darlint be jealous, so much that you will do something desperate.'

So Bywaters killed Percy Thompson, and the jury and the public took the view that Edith Thompson was a wicked older woman with power over her lover. Though she may never have intended her husband's murder, she was convicted; in effect, she was sentenced to death for adultery.

On the morning of 9 January 1923 the lovers were hanged at the same time, Bywaters in Pentonville, Edith Thompson at Holloway. The public was appalled when details of her hanging became known: by the day of execution she had retreated so far into fear and panic that she had to be heavily drugged, then carried to the scaffold.

John Christie

John Christie was one of two tenants at 10 Rillington Place in North Kensington who were each convicted of murder and hanged. The first was Timothy Evans; after his wife and baby daughter were found dead at the house, the dull-witted Evans was arrested, and confessed to strangling both of them. When he was tried at the Old Bailey Mr and Mrs Christie were among the prosecution witnesses. Evans retracted his confession and accused Christie, but he was convicted of the murder of the child and hanged in March 1950.

Three years later Christie left Rillington Place, but within a week another tenant found the bodies of three women behind a wall in the Christie kitchen; under the floor, police found the body of Mrs Christie, and in the garden the buried skeletons of two more women. The women in the house had been murdered recently, but those in the garden had died about ten years before. When arrested, Christie confessed to murdering all the women, killing at least three of them during bizarre sexual episodes. At the Old Bailey he went further, and declared that his evidence against Evans had been untrue and that he had murdered Mrs Evans himself. Christie's story ended when he went to the gallows at Pentonville, but the controversy about Evans has continued to this day. Can it really be true that Evans happened to commit a single killing in the house where a monstrous multiple murderer was at work?

Here Christie smiles shyly with the wife he was to murder. Her body was found with three others hidden at 10 Rillington Place; in all Christie was responsible for eight murders and the hanging of the innocent Timothy Evans.

The hapless Timothy Evans escorted from a train by two detectives. His wife and daughter were found dead and Evans confessed to the killings; convicted of the murder of his child he was hanged. In truth the Evans family were all victims of John Christie.

John Haigh

Another very familiar face in the gallery of postwar killers was that of John George Haigh, headlined as The Acid Bath Murderer and the Vampire of Kensington. Haigh was a killer for profit, who believed that he had overcome the eternal problem for murderers – how to get rid of the body.

In 1949 Haigh was arrested in Crawley in Sussex, by police investigating the disappearance of a wealthy widow called Mrs Durand-Deacon from her home in South Kensington. He soon made a startling declaration that 'Mrs Durand-Deacon no longer exists. I have destroyed her with acid.' In the yard at his premises, detectives found a great quantity of greasy sludge, which proved to contain a human gallstone and fragments of bone.

Even as this distasteful analysis was under way, Haigh was claiming to have killed before: he told how he had shot and dissolved a boy called Donald McSwann in 1944, McSwann's parents in the following year, and then a Dr and Mrs Henderson in 1948. Probably as part of a defence of insanity, Haigh gave a lurid account of how he had drunk the blood of his victims, but it was easily established that he had served prison sentences in the past for forgery and fraud, and had sold the possessions of his victims for thousands of pounds. After just fifteen minutes the jury convicted him, and he was hanged at Wandsworth.

The Vampire of the headline was John George Haigh, who tried to plead insanity with tales of drinking blood. His true motive was probably simple greed, and he took great care to conceal his crimes by dissolving the victims' bodies in acid.

Neville Heath

One effect of the Second World War was to give many men a chance to rise quickly above their prewar social station. The demands of a national emergency softened the rigidities of the class system for the six years of war, and the reward for useful talent and ability, for carrying new responsibilities, was rapid promotion and a leap in social standing.

Among the many good men who carried their wartime ranks into their postwar careers, numerous frauds and charlatans were able to hide. Most gained no more than a chance to impress the girls and boast to the men, but criminals adapt too, and there were many who saw that here was a new way to run up accounts with expensive shops, get credit from banks, and turn the appearance of respectability into cash.

Neville Heath became a murderer only after a long career as a

Special Notice

MURDER

M.P. (FH).—It is desired to trace the after-described for interview respecting the death of MARGERY GARDNER, during the night of 20th-21st inst. NEVILLE GEORGE CLEVELY HEATH, alias ARMSTRONG, BLYTH, DENVERS and GRAHAM, C.R.O. No. 28142-37, b. 1917, 5ft. 11½in., c. fresh, e. blue, believed small fair moustache, h. and eyebrows fair, square face, broad forehead and nose, firm chin, good teeth, military gait; dress, lt. grey d.b. suit with pin stripe, dk. brown trilby, brown suede shoes, cream shirt with collar attached or fawn and white check sports jacket and grey flannel trousers. Nat. Reg. No. CNP 2147191.

Has recent conviction for posing as Lt.-Col. of South African Air Force. A pilot and believed to possess an "A" licence, has stated his intention of going abroad and may endeavour to secure passage on ship or plane as passenger or pilot. May stay at hotels accompanied by woman.

Enquiries are also requested to trace the owner of gent's white handkerchief with brown check border, bearing "L. Kearns" in black ink on hem and stitched with large "K" in blue cotton in centre.

This description of Neville Heath and his many identities was circulated across the country, and helped the Bournemouth police to capture him, though not before he had claimed a second victim.

military and social impersonator. He joined the RAF and was dismissed; posed as Lord Dudley and then was sent to Borstal; took a commission in the Royal Army Service Corps but was cashiered; under a new name he joined the South African Air Force and rose to the rank of captain, but yet again was court-martialled and dismissed. For wearing a uniform and medals to which he was not entitled, the Wimbledon magistrates fined him £10 in 1946.

In the summer of that year Heath murdered two women: in June he left the beaten body of Margery Gardner in a London hotel, in a room they had taken as Lieutenant Colonel and Mrs Heath. Two weeks later, in Bournemouth and posing as Group Captain Rupert Brooke, he met another young woman who was staying in a local hotel, and they were seen to leave together. The hotel manager had reported his guest as missing, and described her escort. Still posing as Brooke, Heath presented himself at a police station, and demanded to see a photograph of the missing woman. Though the body was not to be discovered for several days, the police recognised Heath and detained him.

Heath's motives were probably always a mixture of greed and sexual compulsion. He was a good-looking young man who hid an appetite for violent sadistic sex, for whom the costumes and title were an easy way to become a gentleman, and part of a carefully developed technique for seducing and exploiting women.

Ruth Ellis

On 10 April 1955 Ruth Ellis stood outside The Magdala, a pub in Hampstead, waiting for her wayward lover David Blakely, with a loaded Smith and Wesson revolver in her pocket. She loved him and depended upon him, she had recently had a miscarriage; now Blakely was trying to end their affair, and trying hard to avoid her, but she had traced him to the pub, and as he came out she shot him dead.

She was immediately arrested, and made no attempt to justify her actions or save herself. She told the court that she intended to kill him, and the jury took just fourteen minutes to find her guilty. Even so, the story of Ellis' life that emerged aroused powerful public sympathy: she had had a child when she was still in her teens, in a wartime romance; she had married but separated, then worked as a club manageress and prostitute. Blakely, a younger man who dabbled in motor racing, had first charmed and impressed her then become a drunken, insistent

Daily Mirror

THURS JULY 14 1955

1½ FORWARD WITH THE PEOPLE
No. 16,046

Millions of people are worried about the fate of RUTH ELLIS. Today we ask our readers—

SHOULD HANGING BE STOPPED?

RUTH ELLIS . . . HER EXECUTION HAS SET THE WHOLE WORLD TALKING.

YESTERDAY was not a happy day in Britain. The sun shone but the nation was upset.

At 9 a.m. in Holloway Gaol a woman of twenty-eight suffered death by hanging. Her body was later buried within the precincts of the prison.

Mrs. Ruth Ellis was not a virtuous woman. She admitted shooting one of her two lovers because she thought he was unfaithful. This was the gruesome end to a sordid affair.

Yet who in Britain yesterday felt happy that this mother of two children should lose her life —even though she herself had taken life?

Do the people of Britain believe that the punishment for murder should be CAPITAL PUNISHMENT?

M.P.s would not go past the prison

Are Members of Parliament satisfied that hanging is the expression of the public will?

Some M.P.s were NOT happy yesterday. Some who were to drive past Holloway Gaol on their way to the House of Commons took a different route to avoid the prison.

Five months ago M.P.s debated capital punishment. On a free vote they decided against a suggestion that the death penalty should be suspended FOR AN EXPERI-MENTAL PERIOD OF FIVE YEARS and replaced by life imprisonment.

But did this vote mean that the majority of M.P.s were in favour of hanging? They voted against its suspension — not against its abolition

One man had to decide her fate

How would they have voted on the straight question: Should we abolish the death penalty for good?

How would they vote today?

Because there is a death sentence, one man has a terrible responsibility. In court the witnesses give evidence, the jury return a verdict, the judge passes sentence. They all represent the public conscience. All did their duty at the trial of Ruth Ellis

But one man—a professional politi-cian who happens to be Home Secretary—had to decide whether this woman should be reprieved.

What an unenviable task.

While this young woman waited in her prison cell one man had to decide whether there should be visited on her the retribution prescribed in a pitiless Biblical phrase:

" And thine eye shall not pity; but life shall go for life, eye for eye, tooth for tooth, hand for hand, foot for foot."

These words from the Old Testament Book of Deuteronomy were written probably 2,500 years ago, before the birth of Christ, by an unknown Jewish scribe

And the enlightened British nation today still follows the teaching of all those centuries ago.

It is understandable why people in Britain felt uneasy yesterday. In the rush of life the particular case of Ruth Ellis will be forgotten. But the problem of capital punishment remains

Some murderers attract much public sympathy. There has been more talk about the fate of PRETTY YOUNG Ruth Ellis than there was about the similar fate of UGLY Mrs. Christofi, aged fifty-three, who strangled her daughter-in-law.

But is it unnatural if the execution of a pretty young mother causes public distress?

One fact remains:

Whether a murderess is pretty or ugly.
Whether a murderer is young or old.
Whether a killer attracts public sym-pathy or not—the lawful penalty is death by hanging

Time for a change in the Law?

What the Ruth Ellis case has done is to focus attention on the whole problem of capital punishment

People are asking:

Is hanging degrading to a civilised nation? Has the time come for hanging to be abolished in Britain?

or—

Should hanging be retained as the just penalty for taking life?

The "Mirror" believes that the public should be able to voice its views.

Today we ask readers to give their verdict. There is a voting form in the Back Page.

Please express your opinion on the voting form in the Back Page

Public sympathy for Ruth Ellis was strong. Thousands had clamoured for her reprieve, and the outcry after this pretty but abused and distressed young woman was executed gave strength to the campaign against hanging.

hanger-on. Finally, when she had become reliant on him, he had betrayed her when she needed him most.

Thousands and thousands of people signed petitions in an attempt to save her life, but the authorities insisted that she should die, perhaps because a passer-by had been wounded by a stray shot. There was great outrage when Ellis was hanged on 13 July, and although she went calmly – very probably in a state of clinical depression – to her death, rumours of a brutal execution increased still further the growing opposition to capital punishment. Ellis was the last woman to hang in England.

PART
3

Catching the Criminal, Keeping the Peace

L ondon did not have a police force until the last century. Until then, the only patrols on the streets of the capital were the occasional rounds of ancient watchmen, the only detectives were bounty-hunters who captured crooks for cash.

Jonathan Wild knew in the 1720s what every modern CID officer knows – criminals are caught because they have been betrayed. With this understanding, and his great personal courage in pursuing and capturing the most desperate crooks, Wild's thief-taking was so methodical and successful that he can be regarded as the father of modern detection – it is an irony that Wild was also the most ruthless and powerful criminal that London has ever seen.

JONATHAN WILD, THE THIEF-TAKER GENERAL

> *'I wonder, good People, what it is you would see? I am a poor honest Man, who have done all I could do, to serve People when they have had the Misfortune to lose their Goods by the Villainy of Thieves. I have contributed more than any Man living to bringing the most daring and Notorious Malefactors to Justice. Yet now, by the Malice of my Enemies, you see I am in Custody, and am going before a Magistrate who I hope will do me Justice.'*
>
> Jonathan Wild's plea to the mob which captured him.

Jonathan Wild called himself Thief-taker General and carried a decorated baton capped with a crown as a badge of the authority he claimed. At a time when there was no police force, and the many small bodies claiming to enforce the law were incompetent and uncoordinated, it was Wild's agents who skilfully tracked down the most notorious and desperate crooks across the country and brought them to justice.

Wild was regarded as an authentic expert on crime and criminals: the Privy Council, alarmed in 1720 at the growing number of highway robberies, consulted Wild about ways and means to prevent them. Despite this official approval, Wild's rough and flamboyant manner kept him out of polite society: three years later Wild claimed the Freedom of the City as his reward for sending more than sixty criminals to the gallows, but he was turned away.

It is an irony that the City turned down Wild for the wrong reasons; Wild was a great deal more than just a rough diamond or a social climber. In truth the famous Thief-taker General was a criminal genius, supreme in London's underworld, who had used the law to persecute and eliminate his rivals. He monopolised the trade in stolen goods, and had recruited and employed his own vast army of thieves and cut-throats, smugglers and perjurers, whom he controlled with the threat of the gallows. In 1725 Wild himself went to Tyburn, reviled all along the route from Newgate by crowds who cursed him and stoned him.

Though a coarse man, Wild was shrewd. He knew the law well, and made the most of its loopholes and ambiguities; he had a sharp business brain, and was able to grasp and exploit any opportunity for profit and self-advancement; above all, he was utterly, startlingly ruthless. From Wolverhampton, where he had been apprenticed to a buckle-maker, he made his way to London to make his living as a bum bailiff (an enforcer of writs and summonses, work which involved a great deal of extortion) and a brothel-keeper. He spent some years in gaol for debt, time in which he made useful criminal contacts, and time in which he seems to have worked out the elements of a plan which would make his fortune.

He had learned this two-faced trade from Charles Hitchen, a notorious Under City Marshal: Hitchen bought this office in 1712, but was so plainly corrupt that he was suspended the following year. He had retained his power of arrest and was able to obtain warrants as he wished, but needed an assistant, and recruited Wild. The partnership lasted just a year, but Wild learned how to be a systematic extortioner, how to make more money out of fencing goods, and most telling of all, he saw for himself the power of the thief-taker.

Armed with a warrant and an authority to arrest, an officer like Hitchen could seize any criminal known to him, organise evidence and witnesses to secure a conviction, and send a felon to the gallows. In itself this was profitable, since it attracted a reward of at least £40 – considerably more if the criminal were particularly notorious – but it had a much richer potential. The threat of prosecution made it easy to coerce working thieves into paying protection money, into sharing their proceeds, or into betraying reluctant confederates.

Wild also saw that Hitchen and the other thief-takers were clumsy operators, too greedy in small matters to take full advantage of their position. By handling stolen goods themselves, or taking a direct part in crimes, they placed themselves at the mercy of the thieves whom they should have been able to intimidate.

Wild resolved to make none of these mistakes, and when Hitchen had no more need of him, he set up in business as a public, legitimate middle-man, an honest broker who would arrange the return of stolen property. His masterstroke was to act only as an intermediary, never

JONATHAN WILD
The master criminal. Bold, courageous and popular as a thief-taker, cunning and pitiless as the underworld chieftain who used the gallows to eliminate his rivals, and bring the thieves of London under his command.

holding goods himself, never exposing himself to unnecessary risk. At first by personal approach, later by newspaper advertisements, he offered his services as an agent: victims of crime found that if they followed his advice – bought for a very moderate five shillings – then gave Wild time to negotiate with his contacts, their precious belongings could be bought back for perhaps a half of their value.

The business was a splendid success. Wild had at first run his business from home, but knew the value of an impressive address, and created the grandly named 'Office for the Recovery of Lost and Stolen Property', symbolically close to the courthouse in the Old Bailey. It became famous not only as a clearing-house, but as the headquarters of Wild's thief-taking agency, and the nerve centre of a vast network of skilled investigators and daring manhunters. In the popular imagination Wild was like a combination of Fabian of the Yard and J. Edgar Hoover.

When all the other law enforcement bodies were small, inefficient and confined within their own cities, counties and parishes, Wild's agents travelled the length of the country to bring crooks to justice. For all his fashionable finery, Wild was no mere figurehead, no armchair dilettante. With sword and pistol in hand he led his men in bold raids on criminal hideouts, faced and fought desperate men and was wounded many times – his body carried countless scars and his skull was several times repaired with silver plates rivetted in place.

Wild's operation was of course a strictly private enterprise, but he used impressive titles to add a semblance of official status. When he worked with Hitchen, Wild had invented for himself the title of Deputy Marshal, and carried a baton capped with a silver crown as a spurious badge of rank. He gave his two principal assistants the ranks of 'Clerk of the Northern Roads' and 'Clerk of the Western Roads', giving them responsibility for keeping the roads to the capital clear of highwaymen. For as long as he was successful, catching more criminals than the official agencies, who could object?

While earning the gratitude of so many distressed respectable victims, Wild was cold-bloodedly establishing himself as a dictator of the underworld. His goal was to exterminate his rivals in the successful criminal gangs, his method was to create a machinery of betrayal. A typical coup would be to seize three robbers, and offer just one the chance to avoid the rope if he would impeach the other two – that is, give the evidence against them that would send them to the gallows. That done, Wild would call upon a fourth criminal to impeach his first witness, whose execution neatly eliminated the evidence of conspiracy. His ambitions and his security demanded deaths, and Wild was always ready to give false evidence, to intimate or bribe witnesses, officials and judges.

Beyond this careful strategy of gang-breaking, Wild was almost casual in sending men to Tyburn – he might recruit a youth of good character for a single theft, not for the goods received but to contrive arrest, trial and execution. Each hanging served Wild well; to the respectable it was proof of his thief-taking abilities and earned the usual cash reward, while to his company of thieves it was grim warning of the punishment for any small betrayal.

His success was extraordinary, and Wild seemed to believe that it could be eternal. He expanded his business overseas, renting a warehouse in Flushing to which goods stolen in England could be shipped for anonymous sale abroad, and filled his returning ships with contraband. He became the worst kind of slum landlord, buying properties whose tenants he bullied and exploited. The Wild workforce was busy, productive and obedient: they could expect excellent pay for good work, but only the rope for failure.

This growing empire could not remain a secret, and tales of Wild's other life became common in polite society, but even those who mocked his crude manners were content to let him thrive for as long as he appeared to suppress crime. His allies had ready answers for the critics: hadn't Wild arranged the return of this purse, those documents? Had not highway robbery been much reduced? If Wild were removed, what kind of force or agency could do his work? At what expense to the taxpayer?

Wild seemed to think himself unassailable, and may have gained false confidence from an earlier victory. In 1718 his old patron Hitchen had published a poorly written but savage pamphlet which described Wild's methods in detail, even to the arithmetic used by thief and dealer in dividing the spoils. He pointed out that the thief-taker was in truth a thief-maker, drawing fresh recruits into the life of crime.

But Hitchen's own corruption was notorious, and Wild knew enough about the former Under City Marshal to write a mocking counterblast In the face of a second attack, Wild followed the old principle that there is no such thing as bad publicity, and placed a notice in the press to proclaim himself 'THIEF-TAKER GENERAL OF GREAT BRITAIN AND IRELAND'. Amused by this paper war, the City dismissed it as a personal squabble, and when Hitchen faded from public view his accusations against Wild were quite forgotten.

Wild fell in the end not because of any single outrageous crime, but

INVITATION TO WILD'S EXECUTION
Respectable London had placed great faith in Wild as a thief-taker – when his criminal empire, and his cold-blooded use of the gallows, were revealed, public loathing was intense. This handbill, with its gruesome decoration of Wild's victims, invited Londoners to relish his execution. They came in their tens of thousands.

because public sympathy shifted. Rather like Al Capone in this century, Wild was pursued by the authorities as a major criminal but arrested and tried on a minor charge. Capone died young during a prison sentence for tax evasion, Wild went to the gallows for his part in handling stolen lace worth just £10.

No one factor destroyed Wild and his Corporation of Thieves, but rather a steady loss of confidence which turned quite suddenly into a great clamour against the Thief-taker. Enormous amounts of valuable jewellery were stolen during a state occasion at Windsor; as usual Wild was behind the thefts and as usual he promised that all would be recovered. But the most successful of the thieves insisted on returning his loot piecemeal for high prices, and for many months Wild had to excuse himself to clients who were growing ever angrier.

Suspicions were rising, and old rumours were being voiced again. Having lost support among his prosperous clients, Wild fell from favour with the common people after a popular young thief-about-town called Jack Sheppard made his last, most elaborate and daring escape from Newgate. Thrilled by this exploit, the public made of Sheppard a dashing new hero; when he was taken again after just ten days, hundreds of people of every degree came to see him at Newgate, and at Tyburn the hanging was attended by many thousands of sympathisers.

Sheppard's death was not the end of the public's infatuation. Songs and plays told the Sheppard story, all echoing the theme that 'Little Villains must submit to Fate, While great ones do enjoy the World in State.' This jibe was aimed at all the officials and politicians whose corruption was well known, but Wild was a particular target: Daniel Defoe published what he claimed to be an interview with the condemned Sheppard in which he 'lamented the scandalous Practice of Thief-Catching ... thus they hang by proxy, while we do it fairly in Person.'

Wild himself was in poor shape to protect his empire. The day before Sheppard's escape he had been attacked at the courthouse by a highwayman called Blueskin Blake. Blake was awaiting trial, and asked Wild to repay past loyalty by arranging his release, but when he was dismissed out of hand, he drew a knife and tried to cut Wild's throat. The blade was blunt and Wild survived, badly hurt, but it was Blueskin who gained the public's sympathy all the way to Tyburn. Just when his vigour and guile were most needed, Wild was out of action.

In the next months the authorities searched for ways and means to bring Wild down. Old rivalries between the City and Westminster played a part: the first to begin the building of a case were the magistrates of Westminster, but it was the Recorder of London, an unpopular man trying to cling to office, who issued a warrant.

Although a long and detailed indictment listing all Wild's activities was drawn up, he was tried on two quite minor charges, and convicted on just one. It was enough for a sentence of death. While he waited for execution, his wife tried to hang herself, and Wild swallowed an overdose of laudanum but vomited and survived. Repeated attempts to obtain reprieve and postponement failed, and he was not even permitted the favour of riding to Tyburn in a coach – when the day came, he would sit all the way in the back of a cart. The man who had controlled and manipulated so many was now totally in the hands of his enemies.

'Never was there a greater Crowd assembled on any Occasion, than to see this unhappy Person; and so outrageous were the Mob in the joy to behold him on the Road to the gallows, who had been the Cause of sending so many thither ... Nay, even in his last Lament they did not cease their Insults.'

Surrounded by a violent hate-filled mob, Jonathan Wild died as he had obliged so many others to die, and he was even denied a conventional burial. His wife was successful in retrieving his corpse, but one of the Newgate chaplains betrayed the secret grave to a surgeon who dug up the body, stripped off all the flesh and dumped it in the Thames, then took the bones away. Several generations later Wild's skeleton was donated to the Royal College of Surgeons, and now hangs in their Hunterian Museum.

Wild was gangster and G-man, Public Enemy Number One and Thief-taker General, less academic than Professor Moriarty and more worldly than Sherlock Holmes. His ironic legacy is not as a criminal, for no one can ever again achieve that domination of the underworld, but as the model for later detectives. Every successful investigator must rely on the same networks of criminal informers and the same processes of bargaining and exchange. Although it became a term of abuse for some time after Wild's death, 'a good thief-taker' can be the highest compliment paid by one CID officer to another.

THE POLICE

Despite scandals and conflicts, the British are still proud of their police, and that familiar tall helmet is one of the most powerful symbols of London – a development that would have startled our ancestors.

Even when vicious robbers terrorised their streets, and burglars plundered their homes, Londoners did not want police. When Sir Robert Peel tried to replace the ancient, ramshackle, ineffective combination of local patrols and corrupt thief-takers, he was told that the very suggestion ran against every decent tradition, and true Englishmen declared that they did not want to be spied upon, and they did not want the government to send a disciplined force of uniformed men striding among them to enforce order.

From the time of Henry II, when kings began to impose a new system of justice, with uniform laws administered by royal courts, they needed enforcers, and the first men to take official responsibility for crime control were the Constables. Every year a man was chosen to take local responsibility for law and order, without pay and in addition to his ordinary work. He had two clear responsibilities – he had to do his best to prevent crime by keeping watch himself (and making sure that others kept watch) for crime, and he had to investigate every reported crime. If a culprit could be identified, it was the Constable's duty to arrest and hold him until he could be brought to trial.

At the same time the Constable had to work for the king's courts, to report all crime to the courts, and obey the instructions of a court or a higher district official called a High Constable, for instance to serve any warrants or summonses.

All this must have been a considerable burden, and it was often an unpopular job which men tried to avoid. To help him, the Constable was expected to recruit others to join the watch, and was entitled to the help of the whole parish in hunting a criminal – the 'hue and cry'. By blowing a horn, the note of which was the 'hue', and raising a general shout of 'Out! Out!' – the cry – the Constable called all the able-bodied men and youths from their work and homes to join him in the chase.

If the fugitive reached the boundary of the parish, the Constable was expected to rouse the Constable of the next parish so that the hue and cry could be continued.

The law recognised that the Constable would have great difficulty in

'THE LAST OF THE CHARLEYS'
Even after the creation of the Metropolitan Police, many areas depended for their security at night on the slow patrols of elderly watchmen with their lanterns and sticks; they were known as Charleys, perhaps because their trade was first regulated in the reign of Charles II.

persuading everyone to help, and people could be taken to court for failing to raise the alarm or join the hue and cry. A parish which allowed a criminal to escape offended against the King's Peace, and not only owed a fine to the Crown, but had to pay compensation to the original victim for his loss or injury.

One tradition which has survived is the badge of rank given to the Constable. In Norman times he was given a staff, a ceremonial rod

THE BLACK MARIA
From police station to courthouse, and courthouse to gaol, horsedrawn carriages took criminals across Victorian London. The same basic design, using small separate cubicles to keep prisoners apart, is still in use.

which identified the man and his rank, established his authority and power, and his entitlement to obedience and assistance. Although individual police officers no longer receive decorated batons they are still awarded to and carried by senior officers up to Chief Constable.

In the larger cities more formal arrangements had to be made. From 1285 the law required every city to post a watch of six men at each of its gates. The gates were closed at night, and strangers barred from entering the city. It was the duty of the watchmen to detain anyone who tried to enter or leave, or acted suspiciously, and take them to the sheriff in the morning.

Although the walls and the gates came down, and the population of the City spread far beyond the old bounds, this crude system of watchmen provided London's only official law enforcement for nearly five hundred years. The main responsibility for preserving the lives and property of Londoners was left with the citizens themselves, and this

THE BLACK MUSEUM
For more than a century, the Metropolitan Police has maintained a museum of curious and macabre exhibits – evidence from notorious cases, and oddities like the deathmasks of hanged murderers shown high on a shelf to the right. The principal use of the collection has been to train officers, but visitors such as this Victorian family have been allowed rare and privileged glimpses.

was often held out as the greatest form of liberty. More cynically we might conclude that those classes best able to protect themselves were unwilling to pay through their rates and taxes for the protection of their less prosperous, more vulnerable neighbours.

Punishment not protection, deterrence not detection

London did not want police. Even after the Metropolitan Police had been established in 1829 the people of the capital, of every class, feared the creation of a system of spies and infiltrators, and a repressive force on military lines which would crush the people at the whim of government.

The common fatalistic belief – still often to be heard today – was that crime was simply a fact of life, and that the best hope of controlling it lay not in prevention, not in detecting criminals, but in punishing. Don't attempt the impossible by trying to prevent every crime or catch every criminal, just wait until an offender falls into your hands, and then hang him or flog him or mutilate him in public. Surely anyone who sees such a punishment, or even hears about it, will be deterred for ever from committing an offence?

There would always be hardened determined criminals who were not put off by the old bodies dangling on the gibbets, but experience seemed to show that they would fall into the hands of the authorities soon enough, probably betrayed for a modest cash reward. They could then be executed, bringing their crimes to an end for ever.

Of course, such a system had neither need nor use for a large organised, expensive, permanent police force. In an ideal world, it might be pleasant to abolish crime, but what could police achieve that was worth the risks of creating another tool for government? There were too many strong memories of the times when governments and kings had tried to force unpopular religious or political systems onto the people.

Even so, there were times when crime became intolerable, and those who had shouted 'No oppression' cried instead 'Can nothing be done?' When too many people were robbed in the street, when too many people were burgled, it didn't seem adequate to find and punish an exemplary few – if they could not be protected in the first place, victims wanted action against the very thieves who had robbed them, and they wanted their possessions back.

The early methods of policing all began by trying to tackle specific thefts. They all depended on convincing individual victims that it was worthwhile to come forward, to describe the events, the thief and the stolen property, then taking on the task of recovering the goods and catching the criminal. Just as he might go to a doctor when sick, the victim was invited to consult a thief-taker, either private or public, when he had been robbed. Just as curing enough individual sufferers can prevent a disease from spreading, so the solving of many crimes might reduce crime as a whole.

Thief-takers

Just a few strong-minded individuals proved that crime was controllable. The first was himself a master criminal, the ruthless Jonathan Wild, who certainly mastered the underworld, but only for his own profit. Only slightly more respectable was the magistrate Thomas de Veil. Four years after Wild went to the gallows, de Veil became a Middlesex magistrate. He candidly admitted that he accepted the job because he knew that magistrates could line their own pockets and extort sexual favours from prostitutes. Despite this unpromising start, de Veil proved a patient investigator, sharp enough to become an admired detective, bold enough to tackle organised robber gangs.

De Veil took a house in Bow Street which became his office and therefore the court, but it was his successor Henry Fielding who made Bow Street the centre of London crimefighting: the Chief Metropolitan Magistrate still presides in the Bow Street Magistrates Court. Fielding was the novelist who wrote *Tom Jones* and *Joseph Andrews*, but he also wrote plays which mocked the Prime Minister, and provoked an Act of Parliament which enforced censorship of all plays. Thus made poor, the playwright went to Bow Street to make an honest living.

The Bow Street Runners

Fielding was an energetic man despite very poor health, and in just five years he created an effective force of investigators and legitimate thief-takers. The eighty parish Constables of Westminster were the usual unhappy unpaid conscripts, but from among them he was able to find half a dozen who showed public spirit. These he formed into a small corps which grew to become the Bow Street Runners, the very first body in England to merit the description of a police force. For three generations they remained the most effective police force in the country. Like their Metropolitan Police successors, they worked not only in the capital but across the country, when invited to take up a difficult investigation by the local authorities.

Fielding and his Runners were detectives rather than guardians; with too few men to sustain patrols they could not protect citizens directly. Their method depended on identifying, seizing and convicting criminals; those they did not catch were to be put in such fear that they would either mend their ways or leave town.

SIR JOHN FIELDING
Sir John succeeded his novelist half-brother Henry as the Bow Street magistrate. Although blind, he was resourceful and energetic: his Bow Street Runners used the tactics of the old private thief-takers to become the first official detective force.

Of course the Runners had to achieve their results without the support of laboratories, fingerprint files, or the manpower of a modern police force. Their methods were disliked by many at the time – being little different to those of Wild – and would be in many ways illegal today: they maintained a large network of informers and spies whom they paid by results, achieved many convictions by encouraging accomplices to betray each other for cash, and spent a great deal of their time drinking and dining with a wide circle of working criminals. (Though their official base was in Fielding's house, they carried out most of their business further up Bow Street, in a dubious pub called the Brown Bear.) They also received rewards for any property they recovered, which may have tempted them to prompt crimes which they could then solve.

It was a rough-and-ready approach, but they were so much better at controlling crime than the ramshackle system of watchmen, so much more acceptable than any alternative which would be under govern-ment control, that they went unchallenged until Peel put forward his proposals for reform.

Fielding relied on 'quick notice and sudden pursuit' for his success. The public had to learn confidence in his force, so he placed notices in the press urging them to report robberies promptly. In the same newspapers he posted rewards and lists of missing goods which pawn-brokers should look out for. With each trial and successful recovery of goods the reputation of his agency grew, and it soon became common knowledge that Fielding himself was honest and dedicated.

Henry Fielding drew up a detailed scheme for the policing of London, but died after just five years at Bow Street, before any plan could be put into action. He was succeeded by his half-brother, who had been his assistant: John Fielding too had integrity and boundless energy, and his work was even more remarkable since he had lost his sight as a child. The Blind Beak developed the work of the Runners, creating the Bow Street Foot Patrol.

This was much closer to our idea of a police force which goes watchfully about the streets to prevent crime. It consisted of disciplined armed parties of men who left Fielding's house each evening to make a show of force which would deter robbers. This force was another of Fielding's ideas, which received financial support directly from the government: £4000 was to be provided each year to police the whole of London.

The original Patrol was a body of sixty-eight men, split into thirteen groups, each led by a 'conductor' – of these, eight parties would spread out to patrol the roads leading into London, while the remaining five swept areas within the capital. The men wore no uniform, but all were armed with cutlasses, and the conductors also carried a carbine and a brace of pistols. They were paid a regular wage and followed strict rules and regulations. Each morning as they went off duty the Patrols were paraded at Fielding's office to make a report of all they had seen and done, so that operations could be steadily monitored and improved.

This original Foot Patrol was later supplemented for a while by a smaller Horse Patrol which covered the robbers' favourite hunting grounds on the heaths and open land outside town, but the government was never generous in providing funds and seems never to have regarded the force as permanent. Mounted patrols were successful in reducing the number of highway robberies, but the highwaymen had

BOW STREET POLICE
OFFICE 1816
*In Bow Street the petty
offenders, the drunks and
brawlers, the lowest thieves
and tricksters, were brought
before the magistrate: the
court was originally no more
than a room in an ordinary
town house, and formalities
were few.*

merely been driven further from the capital and many were ready to return when the Patrol was abolished.

Fielding's forces were small, but his approach was methodical, and the techniques of Bow Street men were the operational basis for all the police services which followed. Most importantly they proved to the most fatalistic of doubters that crime was not inevitable on London's streets, and that even limited action could give citizens useful protection against attack and theft.

Colquhoun and the River Police

Time and again London had better magistrates than its miserliness deserved. After de Veil and the Fieldings, Patrick Colquhoun came to town. He was a successful businessman from Glasgow, where he had served as Lord Provost (the equivalent of Lord Mayor). When he retired south he gave his time to charitable work, and as a magistrate to the improvement of the police. He wrote a book which would be the basis for many of Peel's reforms a generation later, but his particular claim to fame is his part in creating the Thames Police. He was called in by merchants who were losing cargo worth more than half a million pounds each year; Colquhoun joined with a sea-captain called John Harriott to shape a plan for controlling the river, then raised the funds to pay eighty men who kept watch on quaysides, searched ships as they unloaded, and crewed a fleet of well-armed barges. The 'Ogglers', as they became known, formed the first London force ever to achieve major reductions in crime by prevention rather than detection.

The example of the River Police, however, seemed to show a new way, and in 1805 the Bow Street Horse Patrol was revived after a gap of some forty years, and fifty-four men were recruited to the first uniformed police in England, heavily armed with sabres and pistols. They were as disciplined as the Runners were casual, and patrolled the main roads into and round the capital; they were joined by a hundred-strong body which revived the old Foot Patrol – though it carried the clumsy title of the Dismounted Horse Patrol – and then a smaller Daytime Patrol. All these units added together were still a meagre force: in the 1820s, the decade before the Metropolitan Police was founded, London had grown to a population of a million and a quarter people, but was still policed by no more than three hundred men.

Sir Robert Peel

In 1822 a new Home Secretary had been appointed, a man of strong resolve who would later become Prime Minister, and who had already made up his mind that law enforcement needed major reforms. He knew what Fielding and Colquhoun had found, and what they had proposed, and with Peterloo fresh in everyone's mind he was also aware of the dangers of letting any military force loose on the people. What London, indeed the country as a whole needed, was a police force which could take crime off the streets without arousing mob resistance.

His was a lonely position: the people feared a new instrument of repression, while the existing officers of the law, from Runners to magistrates, resented any threat to their powers. To those afraid for their liberty, Peel replied simply that '... liberty does not consist in having your house robbed by organised gangs of thieves.' While trying to convince Parliament to accept a wholesale reform, he made changes in the Bow Street operations which put in place Head Constables, or Inspectors, who would be responsible for discipline and the maintenance of high standards.

In 1829 Peel had secured wide support in Parliament, and his Police Bill passed into law. By September the first of his New Police had been recruited and were ready to take up their duties: all had to be literate, of above average height, and able to produce a testimonial from a trustworthy source attesting to their good character.

It was work which would appeal to former soldiers, but Peel was determined that his new force would bear no resemblance to any military unit – the uniform was in a sober civilian style, and each Constable was armed with nothing more lethal than a truncheon, to be carried out of sight beneath the long tails of his coat. The uniform was to be worn at all times, and an armband was added before the end of the year to indicate to members of the public that a Constable was on duty.

The new force was under the command of two Metropolitan Police Commissioners, whose first office was in a private house at 4 Whitehall Place, outside the walls of the Home Office. At the rear of the house a police station was created, which was entered through an old courtyard, a part of the royal palace which had once held a house owned by the kings of Scotland. Officially The Commissioners' Office, the new headquarters was universally known as Scotland Yard.

From their offices the Commissioners controlled a force ten times the size of all the previous police forces added together: in seventeen divisions, north to Islington, south to Lambeth, west to Wandsworth and east to Greenwich, across all London there were within a year more than three thousand officers. Each division was run by a Superintendent, each in turn commanding a handful of Inspectors, between fourteen and twenty-eight Sergeants, and a hundred or more Constables.

The Commissioners laid it down that the higher posts would be filled from the ranks of Constables who would have to work hard and prove their dedication and ability; this was a controversial departure from tradition, when commissions in the army were for sale to the gentry, but enjoyed Peel's gruff support: 'I will not appoint gentlemen who would refuse to associate with other persons holding the same rank ... A sergeant of the Guards is a better man for my purpose than a captain of high military reputation.'

Opposition to the new force was everywhere. All the old officers – magistrates, Constables, parish officers, beadles and the Bow Street Runners – distrusted the New Police and saw clearly the threat to their comfortable privileges; ratepayers objected to the cost; criminals loathed them, and the people as a whole were darkly suspicious. The nicknames for the new force were provocative: though the new force was notably restrained, officers were followed by shouts of Peel's Bloody Gang, and Crushers; they were mocked as Raw Lobsters or Bluebottles for their uniforms.

Worse than the taunts were the deliberate assaults, by working criminals but also by the wealthy young bullies who realised that this new force would not be as easily intimidated, or bribed to turn a blind eye, as the ancient watchmen. One hooligan, Earl Waldegrave, not only joined in an attack that permanently maimed a Constable – they held the man down while a coach was driven across his body – but urged a professional prizefighter to beat another close to death.

It was the new Constables' steadfastness in the face of such viciousness that began to win public support. The instructions to a Constable were explicit: 'He must remember that there is no qualification more indispensable to a police officer than a perfect command of temper, never suffering himself to be moved in the slightest degree by any language or threats that may be used.' These were splendid sentiments, and it is easy to imagine how sorely tempted officers must have been to strike back, but the discipline and leadership within the force were strong. Thousands of officers resigned under the pressure, and thousands were dismissed in the first years who could not meet the high standards, but it is not hard to understand the spirit which was shared by men aware that they were creating something new and important.

One great challenge had still to be faced. Sooner or later, the New Police must clash with a mob, and the authorities knew that the outcome of the confrontation would decide not only the future relationship of police and public, but the government of the capital. These were the last years of outrageous electoral corruption, when Parliamentary voting was the privilege of the few, and pressure from working people threatened to explode in an uncontrollable revolution. The French had sent their king to the guillotine just a generation before, and as always the Establishment was sharply divided into those who would crudely suppress any outbreak with great force, and those who saw that change was necessary, but must come as steadily as possible.

There were two great battles, and failure in either could have discredited the New Police for ever. The first was a direct challenge to the police themselves, when old-fashioned rioting broke out, and the leaders circulated handbills urging a violent defeat of the police which would force their disbandment. At first reduced to standing immobile under attack, the police then attempted their first baton charge. Though it was a confusing and unrehearsed manoeuvre, the charge cleared the streets, and for the first time a mob had been defeated before it could become destructive, with no military intervention, and without any loss of life. A second showdown in 1833 proved that the London mob could not prevail: on Coldbath Fields a large crowd was dispersed by a baton charge during which a police officer was stabbed to death but no one in the crowd was killed or seriously injured. By the standards of the time this was a triumph of sober policing.

Within just a couple of years the methods of the New Police had made it clear that they were not a bullying militia, and earned a reputation for common sense and effective crime prevention. Criminals may not have been reformed or captured, but a great many of them moved out of the capital to find easier pickings in the provinces. To protect themselves, towns and cities throughout the country had to create police forces of their own, on the London pattern.

Criminals may have been frustrated, but the public at large began to use rather kinder names for their police, and to adapt to the new stability: where it had once been quite common for the most respectable men to go armed in public with swords and pistols, new confidence in the ability of the law to protect each citizen meant that the weapons were left at home.

A new detective force

Perhaps the Commissioners were over-optimistic about what could be achieved by uniformed patrols, which could prevent crime but not conduct full investigations. The new force contained no detectives, and for a further ten years the Bow Street Runners continued in their thief-taking work. Gradually some men had been sent out in plain clothes as 'active officers' but there was no official detective department until 1842.

Rather as they had tried to choose model recruits for their first patrols, the Commissioners were keen to select detectives who were very different from past thief-takers, and they certainly impressed Dickens when he dined with them:

> They are, one and all, respectable-looking men; of perfectly good deportments and unusual intelligence; with nothing lounging or slinking in their manners ...

Of all these splendid men, none so impressed Dickens as the stout Inspector Field, who was to become the model for Inspector Bucket in *Bleak House*. Field had been a Bow Street Runner and seems to have been a knowing, cunning officer, familiar with all the rookeries and the people within them. He was resourceful, and delighted in putting on a disguise or play-acting a role to reach his man and make an unobtrusive arrest – presumably a habit learned before there was a strong reliable force of men to back up a Runner in trouble.

Although the uniformed police continued to gain respect, the fortunes of the new detective branch rose and fell: it was not until 1869 that their numbers were doubled, to twenty-four men, and it took a further two years for Parliament to permit the full registration of criminals, with photographs and descriptions; by 1878 there were enough working detectives to cover the whole of the Metropolitan

Police District, and in that year the Criminal Investigation Department was created. These improvements in organisation were threatened by a scandal which did great damage to the reputation of the branch, when three of the most experienced detectives were exposed as corrupt, in the pay of a ring of gamblers. One result of the scandal was that for just a few years the Commissioner tried to recruit detectives direct from civilian life, but this was not a success, and since 1884 all CID officers have been drawn from the ranks of experienced uniformed staff.

Scotland Yard

The original offices at Scotland Yard were much too cramped to cope with the demands of an expanding force. A report in *The Times* described piles of books on staircases, stacks of clothing, saddles and blankets and 'all manner of things ... in a state of what outside Scotland Yard would be called hopeless confusion.' In 1884 a bomb planted by Fenians (Irish nationalists) blew a great hole in the wall of the building, but by then a new headquarters was already under construction on the Victoria Embankment, to be known as New Scotland Yard. This in turn was overcrowded even before the Second World War, but a further move was delayed until 1967, when the force moved into its present building on Victoria Street. Yet again called New Scotland Yard, this is a twenty-storey complex of seven hundred offices, covering eleven acres.

PART
4

Trial and
Sentence

Not every offender went before a court. Although kings imposed their laws upon the land, they reserved great powers to themselves, and sent their enemies to immediate death, or reserved their cases to private tribunals. Anyone declared an outlaw by a court, by the king or by Parliament, even without trial, could be executed without further examination.

Lawyers are given to claiming that our legal system is an ancient guardian of freedom and justice; in truth, most of the safeguards which we take for granted in a criminal trial are quite recent developments, part of a slow progress which continues to this day.

THE TRIAL

The simplest society needed only the simplest ways of dealing with crimes. In Saxon times, when the people lived in small settlements, villagers would seize an offender and bring him before a Folk Moot, an open-air meeting of the older men. The families of the offender and victim would each choose one of its men to speak, and the meeting as a whole would decide guilt. Punishments were immediate and crude – for the serious offences of 'manslaying' or theft of cattle, hanging or a fine were most common, but the Moot might order that a man be made a slave, or have his hand cut off.

Laws were passed down by word of mouth, and each region or settlement kept to its own traditional forms of trial and punishment until about 700 AD when the King of Wessex sent men out to learn about the best of local customs. His name was Ine, and from their reports he compiled a code, 'The Dooms of Ine'. (A doom was a law or judgement – we use the related word 'deem', and to this day judges in the Isle of Man are known as Deemsters.)

Alfred the Great, one hundred and fifty years later, rewrote Ine's laws, not merely to assure justice, but to use a structure of law to unify and strengthen the kingdom under his paramount rule. An offence was no longer a matter to be resolved between victim and criminal, but became a crime against 'the King's Peace'. Grievances could lead to long blood-feuds between families, and Alfred was very precise in his instructions about punishment, leaving little room for local argument or dispute.

A very few crimes were declared 'bootless', or beyond compensation – these included obvious and deliberate murder, open theft, house-breaking and treachery to one's lord. Other degrees of offence were punished with a fine or payment in compensation – anyone who could not or would not pay would be made a thrall, or slave. For any injury there was a prescribed penalty, measured by its effect on the victim's ability to work or fight. Loss of an arm drew a fine of eighty shillings, loss of a thumb thirty shillings, of a shooting finger eight shillings.

Though the concept is strange to us, Alfred was also able to place a cash value on the lives of his subjects; Wessex was a very strictly ordered society, with the king at its head, below him the nobility, who stood in turn above ordinary freemen. Beneath all others were thralls, the slaves who were property to be bought and sold. A life was given a cash value, a wergild or man-price. (We have kept just one use of the old word 'wer', as the human half of a 'werewolf'.) On this scale the life of a noble was worth six times that of a freeman, while a thrall's life had no value at all. If a man were killed, deliberately or accidentally, his family was entitled to receive his wergild from the killer or his family. Once this was paid, the matter was at an end, and the king would tolerate no vendetta.

Trial by ordeal

Judgement by the community worked fairly well in small, tight societies, where the defendant and his witnesses were well known, but for serious crimes a further test was used. Trial by ordeal was an appeal to God to intervene and reveal the truth: under the supervision of a priest, the defendant would be put to a physical test whose outcome was in the hands of the Almighty.

The most common forms of ordeal used fire or water. As a simple test of guilt, a man was required to hold a piece of iron which had been heated in a fire; for women there was a comparable test which used hot water. A few days later the hand would be inspected, and while healthy healing was regarded as a clear sign of innocence, any infection would show that God disapproved of the defendant.

It was not unknown for a bribed or sympathetic official to use a warm rather than a hot iron, and courts could choose instead a form of trial which used water, though this was an ordeal in which it was probably more comfortable to be guilty. The accused would be bound and flung or lowered into a pond or river. If he floated, he was judged to be guilty, but if God allowed the water to embrace him, he was assuredly innocent – if he lived long enough to be drawn back to shore, he won his case.

One of the novelties imported by the Normans was trial by battle, an official duel between accuser and accused in which God would give victory to the innocent. This could not be used where an entire community had made the complaint, or for a woman, and became unpopular with the king's judges; they permitted it most often when an accomplice wanted to gain his own freedom by accusing another. This made it a little more likely that the combatants would be evenly matched, but still gave the strong a powerful advantage over the weak.

We are used to the idea that the state prosecutes criminals, but in the Middle Ages it was the victim or his community which brought the matter to court. At worst, the accused was an accomplice to the crime, who could escape execution if he made full confession and then succeeded in convicting his companion in crime. When trials were by battle, a strong criminal had only to defeat his partner in a fight to walk away free.

Assizes and Quarter Sessions

In the twelfth century, Henry II spent much of his reign trying to strengthen the position of the Crown against powerful provincial nobles and the Church. To enforce the king's laws across the country he decreed that his judges, instead of remaining in the capital, should travel regularly around the country, pausing in important cities to conduct trials where serious crimes were alleged. These were the Assizes (from the French word 'assis', meaning sitting), and although Assizes came to an end in 1972 with the creation of Crown Courts, judges still travel around a circuit to hear cases.

Henry's reform was also intended to improve the quality of justice. As the king's appointees, the judges were intended to be above local loyalties and prejudices, and by sitting regularly they should be able to prevent lengthy and unjust delays. The new system went further. It had been the custom to call together a group of local men to help in deciding the truth in any dispute, the twelve good men sworn to determine the truth. Under the new laws each royal judge was to be assisted by a jury which would decide guilt, and the judge would be obliged to follow their decision. This meant that local knowledge could assist the judge, and gave some reassurance that the judges were not being sent out to enforce the king's whim.

The Assizes were intended to deal with the most serious crimes; less grave matters were tried by Justices of the Peace – local landowners sworn to assist each county's sheriff at courts called the Quarter Sessions, held four times a year.

Even when the barbarity of trial by ordeal and by combat had been abolished, the form of trial followed by these courts was by our standards crude, dangerously lacking in balance, and unnervingly swift. We are accustomed to trials which take days, even weeks, to reach a conclusion, but in those days the prisoner at the bar might be convicted

TICKET TO THE TRIAL OF EARL FERRERS
Any grand lengthy trial at Westminster became a social event as fashionable as a successful play. The prosperous would buy tickets, valid for a day, to see their friends and be seen.

and sentenced to death within half an hour – less time than our courts spend on a contested parking ticket.

Before the accused themselves were brought to court, a special jury – called a grand jury – considered the bills of indictment, in which the crime and the basis of the case against each defendant had been set out. If a majority of the twelve members of this jury voted that there was a case to answer, the indictment became the accusation which the defendant must face.

The accused, who might have been waiting months for the court session, were then brought from the gaol chained together in batches. Once the court was ready to hear the indictments – that is, the documents stating what crime had been committed, and the basis of the case against each defendant – each prisoner in turn would have his irons struck off, and be brought to the bar of the court to enter a plea. Failure to enter a plea prevented the trial from proceeding, but the authorities had powers which forced pleas from all but the bravest prisoners. (This is described in **The Press Yard** on pages 177–178). When the usual Not Guilty plea had been entered – usual because the punishment for almost all serious crimes was death – the twelve members of the trial jury would be sworn in from a panel provided by the sheriff.

The trial itself began with the witnesses for the prosecution, who would each be called, placed on oath to tell the truth, and say their piece. At this point arguments between defendants and witnesses were common: the accused himself was not permitted to use a lawyer except to argue a specific point of legal interpretation. When all the witnesses had been heard, the jury gave its verdict, which had to be unanimous for a conviction. A defendant who was acquitted was discharged; if convicted he would be remanded for sentence.

This form of trial was short because it lacked several elements which we would now regard as essential to a fair hearing. Although judges often allowed prisoners to use the services of a lawyer after the 1730s, there was no legal right to counsel until 1836; the defence was not at first allowed to produce witnesses, and even then they were not allowed to swear on oath until 1702. The defence could not take sworn statements from witnesses to use before the trial, or compel them to attend, until 1867 – though both of these facilities had long been available to the prosecution.

Rules of evidence which protect the defendant, and which we take for granted, did not appear until the eighteenth century. Hearsay, usually no more than gossip, was permitted, and there was no requirement that the evidence of an accomplice be properly corroborated. This was particularly important when a partner in crime could not only save his own neck by lying, but make sure that he received the reward of £40 for sending his companion to the gallows. The jury did not have the opportunity to hear a balanced account – prosecution witnesses all solemnly swore to tell the truth, but prisoners were not allowed to give their evidence on oath until 1898.

A surprising number of cases did end in acquittal, but not always for good reason: denied a chance to speak for himself, or hire a lawyer to speak for him, even an innocent defendant might try to buy an acquittal or look for a way to get the charge reduced so that he would not hang. If he could not bribe the prosecutor or the judge, the prisoner might hope to load the jury. Each defendant was allowed to reject up to thirty-five possible jurors without giving a reason, and more if he could show why they were unsuitable. A clever defendant could hope to include some who would favour him, or who might be open to bribe or threat. Once defence witnesses were permitted, an uneasy defendant might hire a witness from among the 'straw men', the professional perjurers ready to lie for cash. These were easily identified, as they paraded outside the court, by the wisp or two of straw stuck into their shoe buckles to advertise their trade. They often used one trick which reveals the power of the oath: while making a living from false evidence they were prepared to risk punishment but not damnation. As they brought the Bible to their lips to swear, it was the thumb, not the book, that was kissed.

The verdict

Hanging was the only sentence allowed by law for a vast range of minor crimes, and trials gave prisoners little chance to offer a convincing defence, but even the most hardened Londoners shrank from sentencing to death every petty thief and trivial offender brought to court. When their pity was aroused by the prisoner, or their common sense affronted by the proceedings, they simply refused to convict on capital charges. Juries acquitted even when the evidence was apparently overwhelming, or chose to convict on a lesser charge for which benefit of clergy was available, to save the prisoner's life.

This was most blatant where the law set a fixed value of stolen goods above which the prisoner must die. The jury would set a lower price on the goods: in one famous case a jury valued twenty-three guineas at thirty-nine shillings, an absurdity which brought the theft one shilling below the level of a hanging matter. Judges sometimes applied pressure, by fining jurors or bringing them before other courts to answer for their decisions, but in the late seventeenth century such coercion was forbidden. In fact, judges themselves would sometimes lower charges, or spell out to the jury how they might bring in a non-capital verdict.

The Neck Verse

Have Mercy on me, O God, according to Thy steadfast love; according to Thy abundant mercy blot out my transgressions.
The first verse of the 51st Psalm – the Neck Verse.

With twenty words, thousands of prisoners saved themselves from the rope, using a legal loophole which dated back to the thirteenth century. Henry II had tried to impose royal justice across the realm, but after the murder of Becket the Church kept the right to administer religious law in Church courts: any priest, or clerk in holy orders who stood accused of a crime could insist on being handed over to the Church. Since Henry had also reintroduced the death penalty, while Church courts imposed only light punishments, it was a very valuable privilege.

At first, any claim to 'benefit of clergy' required strong proof, but in time judges realised that clerical privilege was a useful way of dealing with cases in which death was the only sentence permitted by law, but hanging seemed much too harsh a punishment. The requirements were steadily reduced, until just one remained – the ability to recite the neck verse.

Some prisoners were able to read the verse, but many more memorised it and were rehearsed in it by their gaolers until they were word-perfect. Defendants faltered as they pretended to read aloud in court, but it didn't matter: by the end of the sixteenth century half the men convicted of felony were recorded as having successfully claimed benefit of clergy.

The privilege allowed courts to be merciful, but there was a risk that dangerous criminals would be able to escape serious punishment time and again. The law was changed so that a convict might claim benefit of clergy just once, but would then be branded on the left hand to prevent future claims; in fact, a simple bribe was usually enough to ensure that the branding iron was applied too quickly or too cold to leave a clear mark.

For three centuries fresh laws removed benefit of clergy from most offences, and transportation and imprisonment were used to provide more workable alternatives to hanging, but the privilege was not finally abolished until 1827.

The Press Yard

> *'That he be put into a mean house, stopped from any light, and be laid upon his back with his body bare; that his arms be stretched forth with a cord, the one to one side, the other to the other side, and in like manner his legs be used; and that upon his body be laid as much iron and stone as he can bear, and more. The first day he shall have three morsels of barley bread, and the next he shall drink thrice of the water in the next channel to the prison door, but not of spring or fountain water; and this shall be his punishment till he die.'*
>
> Lord Chief Justice Glynn, sentencing Major Strangwayes in 1657. The Major's friends cut short his agony by standing upon his chest until he died.
> His case is described on pages 108–110.

For more than five hundred years any defendant who refused to accept a trial in an English court could be tortured, if necessary unto death. The authorities faced a legal problem if a defendant refused to say whether he was guilty or innocent, because Magna Carta had provided that no freeman should be punished 'except by the lawful judgment of his peers'. This had been written to establish jury trial, to prevent kings and powerful nobles from using courts to harm their enemies, but was interpreted to mean that anyone who refused a jury trial could not be punished.

The law's original intention was that anyone refusing in this way would be left in harsh imprisonment to reconsider, but by a macabre misunderstanding it was interpreted to mean harsh penance, and in time the common way of imposing this penance was to crush the defendant under heavy weights.

Between Newgate Prison and the courthouse in the Old Bailey was a broad space, the Press Yard, which fronted both the most luxurious and expensive apartments for wealthy prisoners and the Press Room. Here the defiant accused would be spread out, and a board rather like a door placed on top of him. This board would then be loaded with stones, iron blocks or other heavy weights until either he chose to plead or he was fatally crushed. A milder alternative used from time to time was to bind together the thumbs of some defendants to cause great pain, but anyone resisting this could still be pressed.

It may seem reasonable to ask just why anyone would choose such a painful death, especially when extra refinements were sometimes used, such as placing a sharp stone under his back, or putting a hard-edged piece of wood beneath the board.

The usual reason for facing such pain seems to have been that the defendant wanted his property to pass to his family: if he were convicted of a felony, not only would he hang, but his estate could be seized by the Crown. By refusing to go to trial, especially in the face of damning evidence, some defendants chose an earlier, more agonising death.

At first, the method was to apply weights, remove them, give the man only the worst bread and the foulest water, and re-press him with greater force, and then repeat the cycle until either he was dead or chose to plead. Then some courts appear to have used the press as a means of execution, ordering the immediate use of weights which could only cause death.

Pressing began in the thirteenth century and was not abolished until 1772. There was no sudden move to leniency; it was decided that silence should now lead to automatic conviction, and only later did courts start from a presumption of innocence and conduct a full trial.

THE OLD BAILEY

Defend the children of the Poor and punish the wrongdoer.
Written over the entrance to the Central Criminal Court.

Between the many skyscrapers which now dominate the skyline of the City of London, one landmark is easy to spot. On top of a dome to the west gleams the golden figure of a robed woman – clear-eyed, not blindfolded – holding scales in her left hand, and a powerful sword in the right. She is Justice, and she stands on the Central Criminal Court, above a narrow street called Old Bailey.

This courthouse was built in the first years of this century, but the site has been associated with justice and punishment for at least eight hundred years: this was the north-west entrance to the City of London, and here the road passed under the arch of Newgate. The gatehouse

THE SESSIONS HOUSE IN THE OLD BAILEY 1772
This courthouse stood next to Newgate prison, and in the yard behind the central gate all the defendants, witnesses, false witnesses, legal touts and lawyers would gather to do business as cases were heard with extraordinary speed in the courtroom within.

Front of the Sessions   House in the Old Bailey.

became a prison, but there was at first no permanent court: prisoners in Newgate were simply held until the next visit by a judge – the Gaol Delivery, when all the accumulated cases would be heard.

The uneasy balance of power between the king and the City was maintained when the first judicial body – the Commissioners for General Gaol Delivery – was appointed by the king, but he granted a charter in 1327 which ensured that the Lord Mayor of London would always sit as First Commissioner. To this day, the judge presiding in

MURDER AT THE OLD BAILEY
In 1712 Jane Housden faced trial for coining. When her lover, a highwayman called William Johnson, went to speak to her in the dock his way was barred by the Turnkey of Newgate, a man called Spulring. Johnson drew his pistol, and urged on by Housden he shot the gaoler dead in full view of the court. Both were immediately tried, convicted and condemned for the murder, and hanged days later in the street outside the courthouse.

Court One at the Old Bailey does not take the imposing central seat, but the one immediately to the right. Although the Lord Mayor no longer sits as a judge in this court, the principal seat is reserved for his ceremonial attendances.

At first, trials were held in a convenient room within the gaol, or if necessary a neighbouring house would be rented, but this exposed the judges to gaol fever. It was to avoid 'vysiting places infected skyns … and much peryll and daunger' that the Court of Aldermen paid £7000 in 1539 to build a separate courthouse next to the gatehouse 'over against Fleet Lane in the old bailey'. A bailey was a defensive wall or earthwork, so the new building was to be raised close to a stretch of the old City wall which ran along the ridge above the Fleet Prison.

This first courthouse – the Sessions House – had just a single court, but since it had been expensive to build, and was needed only occasionally, one of the Freemen of the City was allowed to rent it for the rest of the year; around the building was a garden reserved for the pleasure of the mayor and judges. The court itself was no more than a small yard, open to the sky, and although the judges sat on a kind of

WAINWRIGHT ON TRIAL
This is the Old Bailey of the 1870s, and in the dock sits Henry Wainwright, a murderer whose crime excited the Victorian taste for grotesque drama. Wainwright was a businessman and prominent churchgoer who shot a woman, but his crime was not discovered until a year later when his curious assistant opened a parcel to find the victim's severed head.

balcony within the building, defendants and witnesses waited their turn exposed to the weather.

It must have been very difficult to conduct even the very brief trials of that time, and acquittal did not guarantee release – many of the prisoners still owed fees to the Newgate Keeper, and were returned to the prison until the debt was cleared. Spectators too had to pay a fee: the City Swordbearer was allowed to charge the public for admittance, and like ticket touts today he varied his prices according to the popularity of the trial, up to one guinea per day for the most notorious cases (then a good fortnight's wages for a skilled man).

When Newgate was rebuilt in 1774 a New Sessions House was provided, though still with a single courtroom; in 1834 the court became the Central Criminal Court, and was obliged to hold at least twelve sessions each year to ensure quick trial of cases from a wide area around London. A second courtroom, and then a third, were added, and occasionally the Grand Jury room would be used as a makeshift courtroom. Still the pressure of work was so great that courts sat from nine o'clock in the morning until nine at night, served by relays of judges.

In 1877 the Old Sessions House was damaged by fire, and plans were formed to sell that site, and to purchase a part of the Newgate site from the government to provide space for a new and much larger building. Newgate Gaol was closed and demolished in 1902, and the present courthouse rose on the site, as massive and imposing as the prison, and faced with much of its exterior stonework. It opened in 1907, was extended in 1972, and now contains nineteen busy courtrooms.

Nothing has brought home more strongly the closeness of history in this corner of London than recent news film, shown repeatedly on television, of the Birmingham Six – Irishmen falsely convicted of causing explosions – emerging after their successful appeal at the Central Criminal Court. Freed after fifteen years in prison, dazed and delighted, they walked across an area which the police had cleared in the middle of a large crowd which pressed forward to shake their hands and shout their congratulations.

As the happy men strode with their families up Old Bailey they crossed the spot where the scaffold used to be erected outside Newgate, the gallows on which Michael Barrett was hanged more than one hundred and thirty years before. The last person to be executed in public in Britain, Barrett was an Irish nationalist convicted of planting a deadly bomb.

THE JURY

The Modern and Simplified Jury Oath

I swear by Almighty God that I will faithfully try the defendant
and give a true verdict according to the evidence

How can anyone know the truth? This person says one thing, the other
person the opposite, there are witnesses but we don't know whether
they are biased or bribed or simply have bad memories.

Courts throughout the Christian world faced a difficult choice when,
in 1215, the Lateran Council rule out ordeal as a form of trial. It was at
this point that many countries turned to torture, trying to establish
guilt by confession; in England, and some other countries such as
Denmark, the choice was to let questions of innocence be decided by a
panel of people from the neighbourhood – a jury.

Before there were juries as such, any person accused of a crime had to
get his neighbours to take oaths to a court that he was known to them
as an honest man – if there were enough of them, and particularly if
they were witnesses of some power or influence, he would walk free.
The idea of judgement by a panel of other ordinary people – rather than
by a local nobleman or one of the king's judges – was intended not only
to use the jury's common sense, but their direct knowledge of the
neighbourhood, and probably the victim and the offender. This was
useful in criminal cases, and helped to resolve other disputes about
inheritance or land boundaries, when they could use that local
knowledge to establish what had been said, what had been done, and
what was fair.

The use of juries was at first very much a matter of local custom, used
by nobles, and then by the king's sheriffs, but when Henry II transferred
the work of trying and punishing criminals to his own courts, he
incorporated the use of sworn juries.

There were originally two levels of jury in criminal cases – a Grand
Jury which made a first examination to see if there was a case to answer,
and a Petit Jury, which would convict or acquit after hearing the full
evidence. A further odd and specialised jury was empanelled if a woman
convicted of a capital crime claimed that she was pregnant – this jury

would consist only of matrons, and would decide whether the prisoner was indeed carrying a live child. If so, the luckless woman would not be hanged until after the child's birth.

We are now used to the idea that juries are able to speak for the common people, to help prevent injustice; every year there are jury decisions which may infuriate the government, but must be accepted – only in time of war or a state of emergency can the use of juries be suspended.

It was not always that way. For some crimes, like treason, no trial was necessary once a man had been declared an outlaw and it was an easy matter for kings to contrive to have cases against their enemies heard in special and secret courts such as the Star Chamber. Even when a jury sat on a case, it was very ordinary for a sheriff to select carefully a jury that would do his bidding, to bribe them, or to intimidate them if they showed signs of making up their own minds. They could be held 'without meat, drink, fire and candle' until they gave in; if they still resisted the pressure, they could be placed in a cart and towed through the streets to be abused and pelted with rubbish by hired rowdies.

Juries had no clear right to bring in the verdict according to their consciences until 1670, when the courage of an Old Bailey jury in one extraordinary case outfaced a corrupt and vicious court. The accused in the case were two Quakers who had preached to a meeting in the City (at a time of great persecution for Quaker beliefs), and they were subjected to atrocious treatment during their trial, including threats to cut out their tongues if they persisted in contesting points of law.

The jury was very strongly instructed to bring in guilty verdicts, but they found just one defendant guilty of one lesser charge. They were plainly outraged by the trial, but performed their task conscientiously: they did not simply throw out all the charges, but decided to give their honest opinion on each alleged offence.

The reaction of the court was one of fury: the Lord Mayor ordered the jury to be locked up overnight without food or warmth. When they refused to change their verdict next day, it was The Recorder who shouted at them 'We shall have a positive verdict or you shall starve for it!' During the following days and nights the jury held firm, even though they were each fined 'for going contrary to plain evidence' then gaoled in Newgate for failing to pay. In the end just four remained in custody for several months until they won an appeal to the Lord Chief

Justice, and only then to obtain damages from the trial court for their suffering. Of those two original Quakers, one went on to great fame – he was William Penn, who later emigrated to America and founded the state which still bears his name, Pennsylvania. The jurors' names are not so famous, but their courage is recorded on a plaque in the main hall of the Central Criminal Court at the Old Bailey.

There have been repeated threats to the jury system, from those who are sure that ordinary citizens are too stupid or too gullible to be trusted with serious and complex cases, but it has managed to survive. It is true that in many other countries the use of juries is more limited, but this is usually where the judiciary is a separately trained profession kept well apart both from government and the lawyers who plead cases. It is in just those cases where it fears that the state is acting too harshly, or that the lawyers have reached too cosy an arrangement, that the jury is at its best.

THE HANGING JUDGE

George Jeffreys was an able and ambitious lawyer who became Common Serjeant at the age of twenty-three, Recorder of London at thirty-three, Lord Chief Justice at thirty-eight, and at forty became the youngest man ever to be appointed Lord Chancellor. He was also an arrogant drunken sadistic bully who took a raw pleasure in the pain he could inflict, and advanced his career by conniving at the conviction of the innocent, and the judicial murder of hundreds of men and women. He is remembered with hatred, by those who know little of British legal history, as The Hanging Judge.

Jeffreys was the son of a royalist landowner, well educated, but needing to make his own fortune when he was called to the Bar. He soon gained a reputation as a bold and forceful advocate who was never very learned, but was quick to grasp the essentials of a case: he was a skilled cross-examiner, his speeches were powerful and blustering, and carried juries. Knowing that talent alone is never enough, Jeffreys made sure to court the favour of powerful lawyers and City dignitaries, and he was appointed a permanent Old Bailey judge.

Still ambitious, Jeffreys became an ally and drinking partner of Will

Chiffinch, the king's spymaster, undertook secret investigations for him, and secured the friendship of the king's mistress. Yet again he was rewarded: after five years he was knighted:

George from the Courts has Knighthood got
Bestowed upon him for his bawling
A royal mark for caterwauling.

The King prompted a reshuffling of judicial posts to leave a vacancy for Jeffreys: he was to be the new Recorder of London, and then Chief Justice of Chester. This was a valuable appointment, but in Chester Jeffreys was far from his influential friends, and during his very first circuit aroused a great deal of local hostility. A local Whig MP reported to the House of Commons that the new Chief Justice was slack and inefficient, and 'behaved himself more like a jack-pudding than with the gravity that beseems a judge'; Jeffreys made fun of defendants, interrupted witnesses and made jokes at their expense; drank every night, went to bed drunk, and 'in the mornings he appeared with the symptoms of a man that overnight had taken a large cup.' Parliament voted to dismiss Jeffreys, and although King Charles II took no action against him, Jeffreys knew that he had lost vital support and resigned as Recorder of London.

It was courtroom success which brought Jeffreys back into the limelight and back into royal favour: he was the Crown Prosecutor who sent to the gallows a man who had made scandalous allegations in court about the king's brother, the Duke of York. It had been a tricky case, and for his loyalty to the king's interests, Jeffreys was appointed chairman of the Justices of the Peace for Middlesex; this was a county known for its strong anti-royal nonconformism, and Jeffreys set his Constables to break up services, to imprison ministers and congregations.

King Charles faced the threat of insurrection by Whig landowners, but tried to act within at least the forms of law, and avoid the use of arbitrary powers and simple force. Jeffreys was dedicated and ingenious in finding ways to use the law to punish the enemies of the king and the Duke of York: he was prepared to put all his skills and energy directly into their hands, a sharp and heavy legal sword to hack through opposition.

All this was pleasing to the king, and we know that he carefully considered promoting Jeffreys, only to be deterred by the judge's loutish reputation. A single case changed his mind, when Jeffreys prosecuted Lord William Russell, one of the Rye House plotters: Jeffreys was courteous, calm, patient and eloquent. This was a fair trial in which at least one of the judges was sympathetic to Russell, the jury was not loaded in advance, and the witnesses had not been bought. Jeffreys must have known that a vicious or coarse attack might provoke the jury into an acquittal even against strong evidence, and his restraint was rewarded: Russell was swiftly convicted, and went to the block.

Jeffreys' moderation removed the last doubts in the king's mind – within three months Jeffreys had joined the Privy Council and was promoted to Lord Chief Justice. He swiftly returned to his old bullying and abrasive style, crushing any 'flowers of eloquence' from advocates, and reducing his fellow judges to silence. He was already suffering great pain from a growing stone in his bladder.

Jeffreys appeared to take a personal and savage pleasure in punishment. Once, having sentenced a woman to be flogged, he summoned the common hangman for further instructions: 'Hangman, I charge you pay particular attention to this lady. Scourge her soundly, man; scourge her till the blood runs down. It is Christmas – a cold time for madam to strip. See that you warm her shoulders thoroughly.'

When he was not acting the tyrant in court, his ability to seize the essentials in a case served him well, but in any case affecting the king or his interests the ferocity returned. He joined in schemes which brought prominent Whigs to court on all manner of charges, where Jeffreys ensured conviction and severe punishment, taking plain satisfaction in sentencing. To a defendant who protested that he wanted the benefit of the law, and no more, Jeffreys replied 'That you shall have, by the grace of God –' and gave the order for execution the following Friday '– You shall have the full benefit of the law.'

Where the law did not provide for a death sentence Jeffreys imposed fines so vast they could not be met in a lifetime, and gaoled the defendants until they paid. He presided over the trial of Titus Oates, whose courtroom lies had sent dozens of Catholics to their deaths – seven of them condemned by Jeffreys himself. Jeffreys summed up to the jury that Oates' '... depraved mind, the blackness of his soul, the baseness of his actions, ought to be looked upon with such horror and detestation as to think him unworthy any longer to tread upon the face of God's earth.' Perjury was not a capital offence, so Jeffreys ordered that Oates be whipped by the common hangman from Aldgate to

GEORGE JEFFREYS – THE HANGING JUDGE
Jeffreys at the age of thirty-three, already Recorder of London and the most senior judge at the Old Bailey, already striking fear into the prisoners who appeared before him.

Newgate, and just two days later from Newgate to Tyburn. This was plainly meant to kill him, but Oates survived an ordeal of more than two thousand lashes.

Shortly before Oates' trial King Charles had died, to be succeeded by his brother the Duke of York, crowned James II. The death of Charles prompted a rising led by the old king's illegitimate son the Duke of Monmouth, and it was his ruthless extermination of the rebels which gave Jeffreys his lasting notoriety..

The Monmouth Rebellion was a short and untidy affair. The Duke set sail from exile in the Netherlands with just eighty-three men, few arms and little money. He landed in Dorset, where republican Protestant feelings were strong, gathered a small force with little experience of soldiering, and hoped that news of his arrival would encourage other regions to join a major rebellion. The adventure came to a rapid and inglorious end. The preparations had long been known to the English government, who rooted out his sympathisers in London and dispatched an army westwards. Within a month the rebel army had been defeated at Sedgemoor, and the Duke was captured.

As soon as it heard of his landing, Parliament had condemned Monmouth to death for high treason, and only a pardon from James could save him. No longer the 'brave and lovely hero' greeted by the West Country crowds, Monmouth begged for an interview with the King, and when it was granted he grovelled for his life, weeping and crawling to hug the king's knees. Two days later he went to the block on Tower Hill, and although he pressed six guineas to the executioner to do his work well, he was beheaded very messily.

The Bloody Assizes

King James now launched a campaign of raw revenge against the rebellious West Country. The Lord Chief Justice was sent on a mission not only to punish the rebels but to strike fear into the entire region, to intimidate any sympathisers. When Jeffreys left London with an entourage of lawyers, clerks and servants, he was protected by an escort of cavalry and bore the military rank of lieutenant-general.

In just nine days of court hearings, from Dorchester to Taunton, to Exeter, to Bristol, to Wells, Jeffreys dealt with over 1700 rebels. Three hundred were condemned to death, eight hundred ordered for transportation, many others whipped. To speed the process it was made clear that although those pleading guilty might be shown mercy, anyone convicted after trial could expect only swift death.

It was not only the scale of the vengeance which shocked, but the butchery of the executions and the stage-managed spread of public displays across the entire region: officials in numerous towns large and small had been ordered to make ready. They were to erect a gallows, and procure ropes for hangings, axes and cleavers for quartering, wood 'to burn the bowels of the traitors', cauldrons to boil the heads and quarters, salt and tar to preserve them, spears and poles to fix them.

Jeffreys earned hatred not only for the outrageous scale of his work, and the wickedness of the executions and displays – these were, after all, in obedience to the king's wishes – but for the obvious personal satisfaction that he took, and his shows of rage and contempt. In his haste and vindictiveness he abandoned ordinary procedures of law, and dismissed the need for justice. When it was pointed out to him that he had sentenced to death the brother of a rebel, a man who had himself taken no part in the rising, he was reported to have replied 'His family owe a life, he shall die for his namesake.' It was also known that he made profit from his powers, bidding the price of one prisoner's life up to £15,000 (perhaps £600,000 today), but Jeffrey's greatest reward for legalised mass murder was the highest legal office in the realm – he was appointed Lord Chancellor.

For three years Jeffreys then fell steadily from favour as King James manoeuvred to give Catholics positions of power. Outraged Anglicans schemed to place the Dutch Prince William of Orange on the throne, and when William had landed and the king knew all was lost, he deceived and abandoned Jeffreys. As James reached safety in France, his Lord Chancellor was captured in dockside Wapping, dressed as a sea-man, his eyebrows shaved off in an attempt at disguise.

Only by placing him under military guard in the Tower could the authorities save the terrified Jeffreys from the mob. Lodged there for protection, he was effectively a prisoner, and although there were many calls for his execution, he was by now so gravely ill that he was merely left to rot; over the following four months the stone in his bladder and kidney disease killed him slowly and painfully.

Why was Jeffreys such a monster? How was he able to fly so high, commit such atrocities? His enemies have seen little further than Jeffreys' combination of a cruel nature and overwhelming ambition. Historians trying to achieve a rational perspective have pointed to the violence and uncertainty of the times – after all, he was not the only judge to do the king's vengeful bidding – and the extraordinary pain of the illness that would kill him.

Perhaps this is the century in which Jeffreys can best be understood, because we have seen others like him – men whose sadism made them unfit to sit in judgement, but whose fanaticism, obedience and ruthlessness were put to use by powerful leaders. We have seen the presiding judges in Stalin's show trials crush and humiliate defendants whose execution was inevitable. We have watched the newsreels commissioned by Hitler which show Roland Freisler, the Nazi judge, screaming obscene abuse at the Führer's opponents before sending them to deaths cold-bloodedly contrived to be slow, painful and degrading. Jeffreys' defence of the Bloody Assizes, given to a visitor during his weeks of dying in the Tower, has a familiar sound: 'Whatever I did then,' he claimed, 'I did by express orders ....' Hanging Judges are both born and made.

THE BLACK CAP

'Oyez, Oyez, Oyez!
'My Lords the King's Justices do strictly charge and command all persons to keep silence while sentence of death is passed on the prisoners at the Bar upon pain of imprisonment.
'God Save the King.'

The passing of a sentence of death followed a ritual. The jury returned its verdict of guilty; this was sometimes accompanied by a recommendation for mercy, but the law prescribed only one punishment for murder, and the views of the jury were simply passed to the Home Secretary for his consideration.

The Clerk of Arraigns would ask 'Prisoner at the bar, do you have anything to say before sentence is passed?' Again, there was nothing which the prisoner might say that could influence the sentence: the question was merely a relic of the days when benefit of clergy was still a protection against a death sentence.

The judge's clerk would then take a square of black silk, unfold it and place it on the judge's wig – the cap was weighted at one corner to prevent an undignified slide to the floor should the judge bend over his papers – and the sentence of death was pronounced.

THE BODY OF EARL FERRERS PLACED ON SHOW
The authorities were eager to persuade the people that no man was above the law, and having stage-managed the execution of Ferrers they commanded that his corpse be exhibited before dissection.

DISSECTION OF A
MURDERER AT
SURGEONS' HALL
*Fresh from Tyburn, a
criminal's corpse is cut open
for the education of medical
trainees and the grim
pleasure of the crowd.*

We may think of a death sentence as an isolated dramatic event, but up to the 1830s it was the custom to make convicted prisoners wait days or weeks until the last day of a session, when dozens might be brought from the cells to be sentenced to death in a single morning. Most of the judges who passed so many sentences of death in a single morning seem to have reserved strong expressions of feeling for the few truly vicious crimes; attitudes to hanging were then much simpler and harder-hearted. Those were also the years in which pardons were so common that the death sentence did not make execution probable, never mind inevitable, in mundane cases.

By the twentieth century, there were many judges who passed death sentences despite powerful personal misgivings, and some who still seemed to relish their powers. At one extreme was Judge Bucknill, who wept as he sentenced Seddon, the callous poisoner who had murdered for gain; at the other Judge Avory, who responded to an outburst from a prisoner with a sharp 'The jury have found you guilty of a foul and brutal murder. *You, too, shall die!*'

Sentences of death were at first carried out with minimum delay, and then it became the custom to allow a couple of weeks to elapse, to ensure that time was available for reprieve or pardon to be granted, but also so that a prisoner could have some time to bring himself to a proper state of repentance (and allow gaolers to make substantial profit from allowing visitors to see the condemned). It became the custom, by the twentieth century, to carry out an execution after the third Sunday following the passing of sentence. They took place at eight in the morning, and not on a Sunday or a Monday.

PART
5

Punishment

THE BRANDING IRON AND THE KNIFE

> *The Hangman, dress'd like a Butcher, came to him, attended by two Surgeons, and with a Knife, made like a Gardiner's Pruning Knife, cut off both his Ears, and with a pair of Scissors slit both his Nostrils, which were afterwards sear'd with a hot iron.*
>
> An account of the punishment of a forger called
> Japhet Crooke in 1731.

To us it seems no more than savage and barbarous to damage the very bodies of criminals, to cut and to burn them, but these mutilations were at first a Norman reform: William the Conqueror abolished the death penalty which Anglo-Saxon laws had demanded, and imposed instead a new code of punishment.

There may have been a growl of approval from the crowd as the prisoner suffered the loss of a hand, or the cutting away of an ear or a nose, but mutilation had a purpose beyond pain or humiliation: these punishments were intended to carry an unmistakable message. When reading and writing were very rare skills, when there was no police force, no way of identifying strangers, how were respectable citizens to know when they were dealing with a known criminal? If he carried on hand or brow a clear mark of past crime, the warning was plain.

When execution returned, courts still ordered mutilation of all kinds as a general punishment, but amputation was also used symbolically, when the hand which had been used to commit a particular offence would be cut off. Striking a blow within a royal palace – which risked an affray in which the monarch would be endangered – was originally punishable by death, but in the reign of Henry VIII the penalty was reduced. This was hardly an impressive display of mercy, since future offenders would still be fined, imprisoned for life, and have their right hands amputated!

Beyond simple punishment, branding was used to prevent a particular kind of injustice. If a criminal had pleaded benefit of clergy to escape the death penalty, this was a privilege which could be used only once; evidence of identity is always shaky, and the memory of witnesses unreliable – who was to confirm that a man had a previous conviction for felony, or none at all? It seemed sensible to order that a brand be burned, to let the man himself bear proof of his criminal record.

Simple early forms of branding gave way to elaborate codes in some areas, and the 1547 Statute of Vagabonds tried to standardise brands which could then be interpreted across the whole country. All were to be applied to the hand, wrist or other visible area of skin: some marks covered ordinary crimes – M for Malefactor or Manslaughterer; T for Thief; F for Fraymaker, or violent brawler; FA for False Accuser. Other codes betray the concerns of the state – SL for Seditious Libel; SS for Sower of Sedition; K for making treasonable remarks; B for Blasphemer, which in the centuries of religious conflict might mean no more than holding unpopular beliefs. These marks were intended to identify wandering agitators; others were meant to control workers who tried to break away from their employers – V was branded onto runaway servants, to which was added S for Slave should the worker escape a second time.

All these brands were to be applied immediately after sentence: some courtrooms had iron hoops set in the wall to pin down a criminal's hand for branding. The system should have been reliable, but of course it could be corrupted: smart crooks would often pass cash to the executioner, to make sure that the iron would be applied cold, and then stage a vivid performance of pain. Courts themselves often ordered irons to be applied cold, as a merciful symbolic punishment, and it became possible for those who could read, and thus claim benefit of clergy, to pay thirteen and a half pence for the iron to be quenched in water before it was applied.

Despite all these absurdities, and the fact that no civilian court had passed a branding sentence for more than fifty years, Parliament could not bring itself finally to abolish the punishment until 1879. By then, even the army had long abandoned its own marking of prisoners: until 1859 deserters had been marked in the left armpit with D, soldiers of bad character with BC; for these, the military did not use a hot iron, but tattoos of gunpowder and ink.

PUNISHMENT IN THE STREET

THE STOCKS

Stocks were set in market places and at crossroads to display cheating traders and petty offenders and expose them to the mockery and contempt of their neighbours. Standing above the stocks is the whipping post, with its iron loops to hold a prisoner's wrists.

> *The seventh day of March rode a butcher round about London, his face toward the horse tail, with half a lamb before and another behind, and veal and a calf borne in front of him, upon a pole, raw.*
>
> Diary of a Resident in London, Henry Machyn (1554)

When London was quite small, and a Londoner's name and reputation would be known across the City, it was an effective punishment simply to humiliate an offender by parading him through his own neighbourhood. A drunk who abused his wife and children, a bullying

brawler, a blasphemer or layabout – any such minor offender might be led around town, his offences shouted out to the crowd along the way.

There was usually careful stage management of these processions: they rarely took place on the day of the court hearing, but were proclaimed well in advance, to make sure of a large crowd. An offender might be ordered to parade several times, along different routes, or on days when a public festival would attract thousands onto the street. On the day, citizens could show their anger and contempt with shouts and curses, and for weeks and months to follow they would keep an eye on his behaviour, refusing him work, or taking their business to other tradesmen, until they saw that he had changed his ways.

When very few could read and write, street punishment was an effective way of letting everyone know about an offence and its punishment. It gave some reassurance to honest citizens that justice had been done, and gave warning to the dishonest and unruly of what they could expect if they offended. In a time of powerful religious feeling, it was common for courts to order that the offender wear robes intended to show penitence, carry a candle, and pause along the way at churches where he would make loud confession of his misdeed and ask for absolution.

If the crime demanded more than simple humiliation, the offender might be sentenced to be flogged 'at a cart's tail', and for the entire route he would walk with his hands tied to the rear of a wagon, his back exposed to the rod or the whip – this was ironically called 'air and exercise' in underworld slang.

It seemed sensible then to fit the punishment to the crime where possible. A trader who sold rotten goods would be exposed with a sample of his wares tied around his neck, and many a criminal was returned to the scene of his crime – most dramatically, murderers were often put to death where they had killed. At the end of the sixteenth century, when the City authorities were more than usually afraid of the mob, the Provost Marshal was provided with a portable gallows, which he took with him to administer rapid justice to rioters and looters.

A progress through the streets could be a part of a much more serious punishment – condemned prisoners on their way to the stake or the gallows would be exposed in this way, even dragged behind a horse to arrive filthy and broken.

The stocks

Other street punishments exposed offenders, but demanded no parade. Every parish had its stocks, usually close to the trading centre, market place or main crossroads.

The stocks were usually regarded as a minor punishment. The offender was forced to sit with his feet trapped in holes cut through a wooden board, often with the details of his offence shouted to the crowd or written on a placard for all to see. It was humiliating, and no doubt uncomfortable, but an hour or two in the stocks was the sort of sentence that local market courts might pass for giving short measure.

The Pillory

In the year 1560 a maid was set upon the Pillory for giving her mistress and her household poison. Besides the shame of the Pillory, one of her ears were cut, and she was burnt upon the Brow. And two days after she was set again on the Pillory, and her other ear cut.

Time in the pillory was much more dangerous than in the stocks. As the above quotation from John Stow describes, the pillory could be an addition to other punishments, and courts would order that an offender spend several periods exposed, at times fixed in advance to make sure that a large crowd would gather, ready for mischief. Like the stocks, the pillory used a hinged board, but the board was raised on a post to clamp around the offender's neck and wrists, forcing him to remain standing and exposed.

Though a man in the stocks might expect to be abused or even pelted with his own rotten goods, his life would not be at risk; whereas a prisoner in the pillory had probably committed a serious crime and the mood of the crowd could be very much uglier. With his hands trapped he could not protect his head and body from heavy, sharp-edged stones or other missiles: in 1751, two highwaymen exposed in the West Smithfield pillory were so badly stoned that one died within half an hour, the other was taken down so badly injured that he too soon perished. For those who survived, blinding and permanent maiming were common.

The dangers of the pillory could be cold-bloodedly used by the courts. In a notorious Southwark case, a prisoner whose lies had sent an innocent man to the gallows could be convicted only of perjury, which did not carry the death penalty; when the judge sent him to the pillory to face a violently angry mob, there can be little doubt that he intended the man to die. Though he was severely wounded, the perjurer was saved by careful preparations: under his cap he had lodged a tin skull-plate which was enough to protect him from mortal injury.

DANIEL DEFOE IN THE PILLORY AT TEMPLE BAR
Defoe's pamphlets infuriated the government of the day – it was ordered that his works be burned, and the author exposed in the pillory. But public sympathy was with Defoe, and in protest at his sentence the crowd showed rare kindness: instead of the usual rotten vegetables, dead animals and stones, they threw flowers.

FLOGGING BOX
OUTSIDE THE OLD
BAILEY
*From the simple whipping
post, a more elaborate
device was developed, with
an upper framework with
holes to contain the
prisoner's wrists and a
hinged box which was
closed upon his legs. This
stood outside the
courthouse in the Old
Bailey, and allowed
sentences to be carried out
immediately.*

Whipping

Though the most notorious criminals might still be whipped at a cart's
tail, minor floggings were carried out at one of the usual scenes of local
punishment: the whipping posts stood close to the stocks and the

pillories, at crossroads and in market places. A court could order whipping for almost any offence, as the only penalty or as an addition to a fine or imprisonment. It could even order a prisoner to be flogged who had committed no offence at all beyond simple vagrancy: it was enough to be poor, homeless and without work – small wonder that the common hangmen, who usually administered floggings, made a large part of their income from wielding the whip.

There are still those who advocate whipping as a prompt and painful punishment – it seems so straightforward and fitting for crimes of violence – and the abolition of flogging was a long process with many stages. In 1791 the flogging of female vagrants was ended, and in 1820 all whipping of women was abolished, but flogging for men and birching (whipping with a thin cane) for youths lasted until 1948; until the 1960s a prisoner who offended during his sentence could still be sentenced to a flogging.

THE PRISONS

> *… we the miserable multitude of very poor distressed prisoners, in the Hole of Wood Street Counter, in number fifty poor men or thereabouts, lying upon bare boards, still languishing in great need, cold and misery, who by reason of this dangerous and troublesome time, be almost famished and hunger-starved to death; others very sore sick, and diseased for want of relief and sustenance, by reason of the great number which daily increaseth …*
> William Fennor *The Counter's Commonwealth* (1611)

The City compters

Before the first Mayor was appointed in the late twelfth century, London's chief officials were the sheriffs, one for the City itself, one for the county of Middlesex. They were administrators and magistrates, and each had a compter (or counter), a gaol to serve his court – these were large town houses rather than separate strong buildings.

Day-to-day running of the compters was left to their keepers, who ran the prisons as businesses, charging each prisoner for his bed and board, for putting them in irons and for taking the irons off again – in fact, taking money at almost every stage of their confinement. Keepers had no interest in spending their cash to provide any warmth or comfort for their prisoners, and prisoners who could not afford to pay for better accommodation were thrown into a large ward – the Common Side – full of the sick, the dying and the mad, as Fennor describes above.

This penal slum was the lowest level of an elaborate class structure within the gaol: a fee gained the prisoner a mattress, extra rent obtained a private room in the Master's Side; for the wealthiest there was the Knight's Side, or a place might be found within the keeper's own house. The charges for each level were so extortionate that a man might run through all his funds, to sink as he grew poorer from one level down to the next and the next, until he arrived in the lowest hold.

The City gates

Over each of the gateways into the City tall superstructures of two, three and four stories were built; these were originally intended as defensive strongpoints, but there were few external threats, and each gatehouse in turn was adapted to other purposes. Some were let as apartments, or used for storage; almost all were used at various times as gaols.

It was the gatehouses to the west which became permanent prisons, one to either side of the larger Fleet prison. Newgate was much the most famous but for more than five hundred years there was a Ludgate prison. Though it took the same petty offenders and debtors as were confined in the compters and other gaols, Ludgate was a little more comfortable than most because it was used to imprison Freemen of the City, merchants and the well-connected. In 1419 citizens complained that Ludgate was so comfortable that the inmates 'were more willing to keep abode there than to pay their debts', and for a while the prisoners were transferred to Newgate to give them a taste of hardship.

Newgate

> *Newgate is a dismal prison ... a place of calamity ... a habitation of misery, confused chaos ... a bottomless pit of violences, a Tower of Babel where all are speakers and no hearers.*

There were four prisons which successively occupied the same site at the north-western corner of the City, a spot now covered by the Old Bailey. The first was an unremarkable gatehouse much like all the others, with no special status, and much overshadowed as a gaol by the Fleet prison close by. It became a dilapidated ruin, and was rebuilt by the Mayor, Dick Whittington of pantomime fame. This prison was destroyed in the Great Fire of 1666, and was replaced by another large and elaborate gatehouse, lavishly decorated but utterly squalid and corrupt within. By the beginning of the eighteenth century Newgate was firmly established as the gaol for the most serious offenders, those who would be tried at the Sessions House and face a sentence of death.

The last Newgate was founded in 1770, no longer a gateway but a separate and imposing prison; ten years later it was burned by the Gordon Rioters but rapidly rebuilt. Though new ideas for prison design were much discussed, Newgate was still an old-fashioned prison arranged much like a warehouse, doomed to become another slum. From 1783 Newgate gained a fresh notoriety as the scene of executions: instead of being taken to Tyburn, the inmates of the prison's fifteen condemned cells were to be put to death on the open space right outside the prison door.

Executions at Newgate could attract vast crowds, in the street and in and on the surrounding buildings. Often far too many people came for the space available, and in 1807 thirty people, including six women and two boys, died in the crush – many more than died on the scaffold. The behaviour of the crowds was no better than it had been at Tyburn, as Dickens saw when he attended the hanging of a man called Courvoisier in 1840:

> *I was, purposely, on the spot, from midnight of the night before; and was a near witness of the whole process of the building of the scaffold, the gathering of the crowd, the gradual swelling of the concourse with the coming-on of day, the hanging of the man, the cutting of the body down, and the removal of it into the prison. From the moment of my*

arrival, when there were but a few score boys in the street, and all those young thieves, and all clustered together behind the barrier nearest the drop – down to the time when I saw the body with its dangling head, being carried on a wooden bier into the gaol – I did not see one token in all the immense crowd; at the windows, in the streets, on the house-tops, anywhere: of any one emotion suitable to the occasion. No sorrow, no salutary terror, no abhorrence, no seriousness; nothing but ribaldry, debauchery, levity, drunkenness and flaunting vice in fifty other shapes.

NEWGATE
PRISONERS AT
EXERCISE
This picture by the French artist Gustave Dore is the most famous image of the drudgery in Newgate. It is powerful and grim, but too orderly. The prisoners' suffering lay in the chaotic filth, decay and uncertainty.

EARLY NEWGATE
*Every City gate included
rooms which were used for
storage, as apartments for
important citizens, and to
hold prisoners. This is
Newgate when it was still a
gatehouse; the windmill on
the roof is said to have
powered a crude ventilation
system for the crowded gaol.*

Dickens' revulsion helped to change the law; not to abolish hanging, but to hide it behind the prison walls. In 1868 the prison gained an execution shed within one of its yards, where only officials and their invited guests could observe.

We think of Newgate as an ancient prison, but in fact it survived into this century, to be demolished only in 1901, after a bizarre auction of its furnishings and fittings. The scaffold was removed to Pentonville, which became the new centre for executions north of the Thames.

The Fleet

The valley of the Fleet, with its rising ground on the City side, formed a natural boundary and defence, and the original Fleet prison was a fortified and moated castle, more important as the home of a garrison than as a prison. Like the Tower, it was a place where the king might hold his political foes under military guard; over time, it came to be used as a gaol for those who owed money to the Crown, where they could be held until their families raised enough cash to free them.

COLDBATH FIELDS PRISON

As he went through Coldbath Fields he saw
A solitary cell:
And the Devil was pleased, for it gave him a hint
For improving his prisons in hell

The Devil's Thoughts, *Southey and Coleridge*

This was a minor but grim and sprawling gaol, dreaded by the criminal classes and nicknamed the Steel (from the Bastille).

OPPOSITE

JACK SHEPPARD ESCAPES FROM NEWGATE

Jack Sheppard was a very ordinary thief, but a skilled and daring escaper – he broke out of a local lock-up, then fled from Clerkenwell House of Detention taking his plump girlfriend with him, and finally contrived to escape from his condemned cell in Newgate. These pictures show how he did it, penetrating walls and doors, clambering across roofs and lowering himself to safety with knotted sheets. After all this, Sheppard was easily recaptured as he drank with cronies in a Drury Lane tavern.

JACK SHEPPARD IN CHAINS
Gaolers sometimes used irons for security – this is how they held Jack Sheppard in the end – but much more commonly they used them to extort money from prisoners, taking fees for applying an extraordinary and painful weight of metal to wrists and ankles, and for striking the irons off.

NEWGATE IN PICTURES

Most sinister of these views of Newgate is at the foot of the page, the sketch of Birdcage Walk. This was the main passageway from Newgate to the Old Bailey, and beneath its pavement lay the bodies of executed criminals, each recorded by carving initials in the wall – condemned prisoners quite literally walked upon their own graves.

Within a generation of the 1066 Conquest, Norman rule had been consolidated in the capital, the need for a strong army of occupation had passed, and the Fleet became no more than a decaying and wretched prison. The moat was no longer needed as a military defence, and became a stinking ditch into which every variety of rubbish could be dumped, every foul drain emptied. When, it was said, the moat was so clogged by the discarded bad meat and offal from the area's slaughterers that a man might walk across it, it was filled in as a public nuisance.

Although this was still a royal prison, and the keepers were appointed by the Crown, the Fleet was run for private profit, a rewarding business to be bought, sold and inherited. For four hundred of its seven hundred

ELIZABETH FRY IN NEWGATE
Mrs Fry was the last and most famous of the great amateur prison reformers. A woman of strong Quaker principles, she was shocked at the plight of female prisoners in Newgate, and formed an association which provided work and education 'under kind superintendence'.

years, the Fleet was run by a single family, the Levelands. They held a manorial title in Kent which carried the additional perk of a fully-operational metropolitan gaol as others might carry fishing rights. Two of the earliest keepers were women – widows who inherited and ran the family business. The Leveland widows, like other keepers, made their money indirectly: they were at the peak of a pyramid operation, by which every post in the prison was bought and sold, right down to the humble porter. By the middle of the sixteenth century the keepership was changing for £8000, a porter's job for £20.

Providing the revenue to justify these prices was a vastly elaborate scheme of charges and fees to prisoners. A prisoner's only free entitlement was to be locked up in a cellar called Bartholomew Fair, with the vilest, the poorest, the diseased and the mad; payment might yield a place in a bare ward; bedding was extra, a curtained cubicle

THE TREADMILL AT COLDBATH FIELDS

Hard labour was attractive even to reformers as both punishment and discipline, and the treadmill was devised to provide consistent, all-weather toil. There were twenty-six mills in all at Coldbath Fields, one reason why the prison was so detested in criminal circles.

along a wall a little more. The scale extended up to spacious comfortable suites of rooms, for which the charges were much higher than for a rented home beyond the prison walls. Within the prison were a coffee-room and a taproom, both operated to provide income for the management, but there was always room for fresh enterprise, and turnkeys often acted as pimps and procurers. Where there was no danger of political repercussions, a fee would often secure an escape, and the Fleet's most notorious keeper, an eighteenth-century thug called Thomas Bambridge, went so far as to provide a special discreet exit door for that very purpose.

Much worse than all these greedy abuses was the deliberate use of torture. Keepers were entitled to keep a prisoner in irons to prevent escape, but the evil Bambridge and others like him in all the gaols, would seize those prisoners whom they believed could pay well, and load them mercilessly with irons about their arms, legs and necks. Cramped and burdened in this way, held in the darkest cellar, prisoners had to hope that their families could pay for their relief before their health was utterly destroyed: those already weak might well die. Bambridge went to trial for his abuses and contrived to be acquitted, but the evidence of his greed and brutality caused such an outcry that an Act of Parliament was passed to dismiss him.

While the poor died miserably, the rich were able to take advantage of an ancient privilege and serve their prison time in comfort beyond the prison walls. Around the Fleet lay a broad area – fully a mile and a half across – known as the Liberty of the Fleet, and from early times any prisoner able to pay the keeper compensation for his loss of income, and to lodge a deposit as bail, was free to move out and taking lodgings within the Liberty. Safe from their creditors, unscrupulous spendthrifts could live here for years.

The Fleet was too insecure, too corrupt to be used as a prison for serious criminals, but held great numbers of debtors and their families (as late as 1819 a survey found thirty-nine wives and fifty-four children resident in the gaol), and it was the ending of imprisonment for debt which was to make the Fleet redundant. The prison had been rebuilt after Wat Tyler's men had sacked it, the Great Fire and the Gordon Riots had each levelled it, but in 1842 an Act of Parliament amalgamated it with the other great debtors' prisons of the Marshalsea and the Queen's Bench (formerly, of course, the King's Bench), and the grim Fleet finally closed, after seven hundred years.

The Bridewell

Bridewell was completed in 1520 as a royal palace, but within a generation had become a prison for the wandering poor, where they could be flogged and put to work.

Every time a crop failed, disease threatened a country area, or a war came to an end, more thousands of the masterless poor made their way to London hoping to find food and work. Each fresh wave seemed to overwhelm the capital, and among the honest poor were organised bands of robbers and rowdies, drunks, thieves and bullies.

Hoping to give aid to the poor, and reform the louts through a regime of hard labour and punishment, Edward VI ordered that Bridewell should be given over as a refuge and a workhouse. Some might be sent by the courts after conviction, but most would simply be committed by order of a magistrate as 'sturdy and idle': that is, capable of work but jobless.

By 1556 the first inmates had been received and put to work making nails, cleaning sewers, carding and spinning fibres into yarn. It was always intended that those who failed to work would be beaten, but some categories of prisoners such as prostitutes and vagrants were given a whipping on arrival – twelve lashes for adults, six for juveniles.

Though inmates were kept against their will, and lawfully punished, this was not officially a prison. Prisons were squalid and disorderly: this was a new institution, clean and disciplined – a house of correction. Bridewell gained a ducking-stool and stocks, but also a doctor and a school master. It provided health care for the sick, education and apprenticeships for well-fed smartly uniformed children, and was seen as so successful that every town and borough was ordered to provide a local house of correction. Early protests, that it was against the freedoms granted by Magna Carta to lock up those whose only offence was to be poor and homeless, were soon forgotten.

Like the prisons and the lunatic asylums, Bridewell became a place of entertainment for the public, who enjoyed in particular the public whipping of women: these became so popular that a special gallery was erected to hold all the onlookers. Each flogging continued until the president of the Bridewell court decided to call a halt by bringing down his gavel, and one long-serving chairman, Sir Thomas Middleton, was often implored by the sufferers to 'Knock, Sir Thomas, knock' – a cry that was shouted after him wherever he went.

The houses of correction became little more than prisons for petty offenders, and the workhouses replaced them as the last refuges of the desperate poor. Bridewell itself closed finally in 1855.

The debtors' prisons

The Fleet's new partners also had long histories – each had been established south of the river in Southwark in the fourteenth century as prisons attached to royal courts. Both had been used to hold political and religious prisoners during the Tudor conflicts, and had declined to become sprawling debtors' gaols.

The Marshalsea was the prison made famous by Dickens in *Little Dorrit*, as the home of the Dorrit family for twenty-three years and birthplace of the heroine. It was no fortress, but a sprawl of buildings which grew to hold hundreds of debtors and their families – Dickens' own father had been taken there in 1824, to be joined like so many by his wife and children.

When the Marshalsea closed, its prisoners were transferred to the Queen's Bench, another ancient prison which enjoyed a reputation as a comfortable gaol for the wealthy – 'the most desirable place of incarceration in London' – and most of its prisoners in the seventeenth century owed great fortunes. Like the Fleet, it had an area about it in which prisoners could live and move freely, and creditors had the uncomfortable choice between taking a very small settlement or watching helplessly as their money was spent. Useful lodging for the feckless rich stood next to a hell-hole for the poor which 'rivalled Wapping, St Giles and St James' in vice, debauchery and drunkenness.'

Fleet marriages

> *There are a set of drunken, swearing parsons, with their myrmidons, who wear black coats, and pretend to be clerks and registers of the Fleet, and who ply about Ludgate Hill, pulling and forcing people to some peddling ale-house or brandy-shop to be married; even on a Sunday, stopping them as they go to church, and almost tearing their clothes off their backs.*
>
> Grub Street Journal (January 1735)

Many prisoners found ways to follow their trades and professions while they served their sentences, but none more scandalously than the clergymen who turned the chapel of the Fleet Prison into a marriage factory. They charged little more than the price of the next bottle of gin to marry drunken sailors to girls they had met an hour before, noblemen and gentlewomen fleeing angry fathers, and hundreds of couples who never gave their names.

The obscure privilege which the clergy claimed – that the chapel was beyond the jurisdiction of the Bishop of London, came in time to extend through all the Liberty of the Fleet, and in several of the local taverns, the trade continued.

Among all the weddings of secret lovers and drunken strangers, were more corrupt and sinister ceremonies. For the right money, the ministers would backdate a marriage certificate, or help a bigamist by failing completely to enter a record. For a small charge – perhaps five shillings – a husband or wife could be hired from among the local riff-raff; for twice that, a marriage could be registered which had never taken place at all. In these ways taxes and debts could be avoided, but much worse were the occasional kidnappings of unwilling women, among them young heiresses, whose fortunes the kidnappers planned to steal .

Two generations after a Marriage Act was passed in 1754 to put a stop to Fleet marriages, the claims and counter-claims about inheritance were still so common and so complex that the government bought a quantity of the register books used in the prison and the taverns: though it covered only eighty years of weddings, this collection weighed more than a ton!

The Clink

This prison probably gained its famous name from the 'clinching' of the chains in which prisoners were held. It was never a major gaol, and seems to have started as no more than a cellar within the Palace of the Bishops of Winchester. They used it for prisoners who had passed through church courts, and to imprison troublemakers from their very profitable brothels and taverns.

During the religious conflicts of Tudor times, the prison was moved from the Palace to occupy three less impressive houses nearby, and victims of both Protestant and Catholic persecution were held in turn, but the prison then decayed to become no more than a local lock-up. By the time it was finally destroyed during the Gordon Riots of 1780, the Clink seems to have held no more than a couple of prisoners at a time.

Horsemonger Lane

I do not believe that any community can prosper where such a scene of horror as was enacted this morning outside Horsemonger Lane gaol is permitted. The horrors of the gibbet and of the crime which brought the wretched murderers to it faded in my mind before the atrocious looks and language of the assembled spectators.

From a letter to *The Times* by Charles Dickens, after watching the execution of Mr and Mrs Manning in 1849.

Horsemonger Lane was an unremarkable prison for the county of Surrey, adequately managed, but known for the hangings which were carried out on a gallows erected on the roof. Dickens arranged with the artist Leech to witness the Mannings' executions, and they rented a room and a back kitchen which overlooked the gaol for a fee of ten guineas, which Dickens regarded as 'extremely moderate', though it would have represented a full month's salary for many a respectable clerk. Renting out rooms was not the only profitable trade on the day of a hanging – we know that two and a half million broadsheets were printed and sold telling the story of the Mannings' crime and execution.

The hulks

When transportation was suspended during the American War of Independence and the wars with France, a temporary substitute was quickly created. Prisoners were to be confined under guard on moored ships, and put to hard labour on public works. The first of these ships were managed by an overseer who had previously worked on the convict transports, and he received a simple flat fee for accommodating and guarding his charges. He took no interest in the welfare of the prisoners, who were crammed into filthy rotten and damp conditions, and fed poorly: most became sick, and many died.

The half-dozen hulks closest to London were moored at Woolwich, where the prisoners built docks to serve the Royal Arsenal; the ships were obsolete Navy vessels and a frigate captured from the French. They were neither maintained nor staffed with care; during an outbreak of cholera the chaplain not only neglected to comfort his flock, but even conducted the burial services from a ship a full mile away, signalling by a wave of a handkerchief when the bodies should be lowered.

Hulk prisoners – some less than ten years old – were taken from their ships each day for long hours of back-breaking labour. There was great fear of mutiny and escape, so the convicts were surrounded by men armed with carbines, bayonets fixed. At night all returned to squalor, the weak to every kind of danger from their fellow convicts – on one ship the seven hundred prisoners were simply locked in and left overnight under the supervision of a single guard.

After transportation had been resumed and then abolished, long after conditions in many land prisons had been improved, convicts were still held in the same ancient ships. The hulks had been proposed as a temporary two-year stopgap in 1776, but they were not brought under central government control until 1859, when the last prisoners could be brought ashore.

The penitentiary and Victorian prisons

The ancient gaols were foul and disorderly, run for profit, and intended only to hold prisoners for short periods. Successive surveys of conditions in the prisons described unsanitary, degrading conditions. Although there was much tut-tutting, prison reforms were no better as vote-getters then than they are now; respectable taxpayers are never eager to spend on comfort for criminals.

On the other hand, the Victorian public was less bloodthirsty, less convinced that the only thing to do with an offender was to hang him. Juries were always ready to find an excuse to acquit a sympathetic defendant, or make sure that the seriousness of the charges was reduced, where their common sense told them that the person in the dock deserved to die.

Another change of heart was the beginning of a belief that the behaviour of criminals could be improved. Until then it had been easy to dismiss crime as the result of bad blood, or as the activity of a class of people who would not or could not change their ways. Everyone could see how the growth of industry was the triumph of a rational approach –

practical men were everywhere overcoming immense technical difficulties, to invent a future which was transforming the life and the landscape of Britain. Surely crime was just another problem demanding a systematic programme of works?

Harnessed to the advance of industry was a shift of thought: fashions in religion and public morality began to change. There was a new earnestness. The evident transfer of power and influence between the classes brought into discredit the old self-indulgent ways of the landowning aristocracy and the smugness of the established Church, while groups such as the Quakers who had once been mocked and persecuted were earning wider respect.

Social change was a friend to the new morality, and in turn the more evangelical newcomers had a powerful belief in both national and personal change. Just as a man could better himself materially, so he could redeem himself morally, both by acts of charity, and also by long and careful contemplation of the Christian way.

Who could benefit more from such a study than the wretched criminals? But if a prisoner had to struggle to eat, had to be lucky to avoid gaol fever, in a vast ward full of the most physically sick and morally degenerate, how could he be brought to a better way? In some parts of the United States, the idea gained ground that hygienic solitary confinement, combined with constant moral tuition, was a necessity for personal redemption.

Compassion and moral purpose by themselves, though, could never have produced rapid reform. It was a very practical crisis which forced change: transportation was becoming impossible. As the public turned against hanging for all but the more outrageous crimes, governments had shipped out criminals by the thousand. Now American independence had closed Virginia to the trade, and the years of war with France made the seas too unsafe for the development of alternatives in the West Indies and elsewhere. Some prisoners would be held in a kind of exile at home, on the hulks, but more importantly, the Crown would open a great new prison which would not only contain criminals, it would reform them.

The Millbank Penitentiary

The Penitentiary was vast. On the north shore of the Thames at Millbank, behind a moat, it was a mouldy poorly built fortress of yellow-brown brick. It had one thousand individual cells – more than any other British prison before or since – connected by a bizarre maze of miles of corridor, with 'angles every twenty yards, winding staircases, dark passages, innumerable doors and gates'. One warder, even after many years, still kept a piece of chalk in his pocket so that as he moved through the prison he could make marks on the wall to find his way back!

The penitentiary ideal demanded that prisoners should be kept strictly apart from each other, and made to work hard and pray frequently: believers knew that this was the only way to save souls. When it was pointed out to him that strict solitary confinement was driving some prisoners mad, the Reverend Nihil, who combined the work of chaplain and governor in the 1830s, replied 'Health is certainly a consideration, but are morals less?' Nihil was in charge when it emerged that three small girls – two ten year-olds and a third just seven – had each been held in solitary confinement for twelve months. The

MILLBANK PENITENTIARY
The first national prison was built on the banks of the Thames: vast, damp and complex, it was managed incompetently and heartlessly. Intended to stand as a model of enlightened and rational detention, it was an expensive failure, as foul and unhealthy as the squalid ancient gaols.

public was particularly enraged to hear how the youngest girl had begged for her doll at bedtime, only to have it refused.

It was beyond question that the Millbank Penitentiary was an appalling failure. It was too big, too expensive, and prisoners who survived the damp and the outbreaks of scurvy and cholera returned to crime just as quickly as those held in less enlightened gaols. Of course, none of this was enough to destroy the belief that prisons could be used to change prisoners as well as punish them – all that was needed, said the reformers, was a fresh start. Millbank was a mistake never to be repeated, but Pentonville was an example copied scores of times throughout the country.

Pentonville – the model prison

THE MARSHALSEA
Never strongholds and often
no more than ramshackle
collections of close-set
houses, there were several
successive Marshalsea
prisons, used for minor
state prisoners, petty
criminals, and debtors with
their families. Dickens,
whose father was sent to
the Marshalsea in 1824,
made the gaol the birthplace
of Little Dorrit.

Pentonville was the first of the classic British gaols, the original of all the bleak Victorian prisons in crime films and TV comedies. It was planted within a city, surrounded by a high wall and entered through a dramatic gatehouse, to hold its prisoners in small cells along galleried wings stretching out as spokes from the centre. Like the very idea of a penitentiary, the functional design was imported from the United States, but British gaols were designed with a fine Victorian pomp.

For Pentonville the authorities hired Sir Charles Barry – then the most famous and fashionable architect in the land, his new Houses of Parliament rising in Westminster – to provide a massive and ponderous

PENTONVILLE
GATEHOUSE
*When it opened in 1842
Pentonville was the second
attempt – after Millbank –
at a national prison. The
imposing gatehouse was
more than an architectural
vanity – it was intended as
the confident public face of
a design and a regime which
would serve as models for
reformers across the country
as they replaced ancient and
ramshackle gaols.*

gatehouse which would declare the solemn purpose of the gaol as a great public building. The new prisons represented both extremes of Victorian building: beyond the impressive gates were brick cell blocks, bleak as warehouses or mills.

There were such high hopes for this model prison. Here prisoners were to be prepared for transportation by a regime of hard work, they would be fed adequately and clothed decently, and their moral welfare would be guaranteed by supervision and separation. Though gathered in their hundreds, convicts would be kept apart to prevent physical and moral cross-infection. They would sleep alone, work alone, exercise alone in small fenced yards; they would pray alone in small cubicles, and so that they would have no chance to communicate, they would move about the prison with their faces concealed behind masks.

This obsession with orderly separation seems macabre to us, but when Pentonville opened, the Fleet and the Marshalsea were still holding prisoners in foul cellars, twenty or thirty to a room, while at Newgate keepers continued to take fees from a leering public eager to stare at the condemned before they went to public hanging. The problems were very similar to those of slum clearance in our own time – the old prisons were like slum terraces, squalid and disorderly, their replacements were clean, but as vast and impersonal as tower blocks.

THE PENTONVILLE
CHAPEL
*Reformers believed that
separation would help to
reform prisoners: cut off
from each other as they
worked and exercised they
would learn no new
criminal tricks, and could
spend their hours in silent
contemplation of their sins.
In the chapel, individual
cubicles ensured that
prisoners could see only the
chaplain, but of course they
soon learned to tap out
secret messages and pass
notes unobserved.*

Modern imprisonment

The very nature of punishment was changing: sentence of death would effectively be limited to murderers, and transportation would soon end. For the first time, prison sentences would be the normal way of punishing serious offenders, and governments steadily took over the responsibility for prisons from the local benches.

The final nationalisation in 1877 not only closed the worst prisons but removed the worst managements – there was to be a new national body of reliable uniformed staff who would receive a standard wage, under the supervision of governors who would bring the discipline of an army and the style of colonial administrators.

London lost the majority of its prisons by the end of the century: more than a dozen old gaols were replaced by just five large institutions.

The oldest was Brixton, founded in the 1820s; then Pentonville, Holloway, Wandsworth, and finally Wormwood Scrubs, built by convict labour in the 1890s.

Conditions in these prisons have notoriously worsened, as overcrowding and decay have turned them into the new penal slums. Only Holloway has been rebuilt, when it was 130 years old, and just one new prison has been added in Woolwich (close to the moorings of the old prison hulks); the others seem likely to reach their bicentenaries.

A Gallery of Modern Prisons

Brixton

This is the oldest of London's gaols still to receive prisoners. The design was accepted by the Surrey Justices in 1819, and the original buildings form a crescent around a central block, which at first included the governor's house, to give him a commanding view of all the blocks and yards. Brixton was intended as a house of correction, in which prisoners could be put to work, and was the first prison to install a treadwheel: convicts walked on the slatted steps of a large drum, turning a shaft which powered a cornmill.

It is remarkable that although Brixton will still be used well into the twenty-first century, it was sold for demolition one hundred and forty years ago! With its small cells and constant overcrowding, Brixton was far from satisfactory, and the county authorities sold the entire gaol at a great loss in 1852. The buyer planned to pull it down and make his profit on the reclaimed materials, but accepted a good offer from the Prison Commissioners, who wanted to establish a new women's prison.

For its new role the gaol was expanded to its present size, with new cell blocks, a chapel and a laundry in which the women would work. For about twenty years Brixton became a military prison, but in 1897 it was returned to civilian use, and took the role which it has kept ever since, as the principal remand prison for London.

Holloway

The original Holloway was an extravagant high Victorian architectural fantasy: when the City of London wanted to provide a new house of correction in the 1840s, it chose to follow the new convention of a radial design, but to erect in front of it 'a noble building of castellated Gothic' – a medieval fortress, dominated by a replica of Caesar's Tower at Warwick Castle.

Taken into the state system in 1877, Holloway became a prison for women at the turn of the century, and became notorious for its treatment of suffragettes. In the Second World War it became an internment prison for enemy aliens and potential traitors like Sir Oswald and Lady Mosley, but by the war's end it had returned to its old civilian function.

Just three women were executed at Holloway. Edith Thompson was hanged in 1923 for the murder of her husband, at the same time as her lover and accomplice went to the gallows half a mile away at Pentonville. In the 1950s two women were hanged who had committed murders within ten months of each other, just two hundred yards apart in the same Hampstead street: we remember Ruth Ellis as the last woman to be executed in Britain, but she closely followed the wretched

PRISONERS IN THE
BROAD ARROW –
WORMWOOD SCRUBS
1890
Convict arrows have become a cartoonist's cliché, but in fact they were used for only fifty years, and removed as long ago as 1922. The mark was originally used on a wide range of government stores by the Earl of Albany in 1700, and was taken from the pheon, or broad arrow, of his own coat of arms.

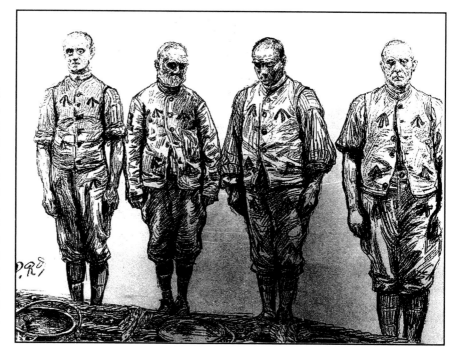

THE OLD HOLLOWAY
PRISON
*City of London archives
show us how the architect
J B Bunning seduced the
Corporation into building
this grandiose High
Victorian prison as a
replacement for its old plain
gaols. The simple cell blocks
hid behind an elaborate
gatehouse, and beneath a
fanciful centre block which
copied Warwick Castle.*

and disturbed Mrs Christofi, whose maternal jealousy led to the murder of her daughter-in-law.

The splendid old Holloway was demolished in the 1970s, to make way for a miserably ordinary modern gaol. Officials shiftily arranged for the flamboyant gatehouse to be pulled down before any protest could be mounted.

Wandsworth

To speak plainly, the exterior ... is mean and ill-proportioned to the last degree . . . all the bad taste of Cockney-Italian villas ... the stunted gateway is heavy even in clumsiness, and the whole aspect of the structure uncommanding as a Methodist college.
The Criminal Prisons of London, Henry Mayhew (1856)

The Surrey authorities sold Brixton and two other smaller gaols, and built Wandsworth as a new and efficient house of correction for short-term prisoners. It was on a grand scale, with two separate radial blocks to hold both male and female prisoners – the majority of men spent their days pointlessly turning the crank handles of hard-labour machines in their cells, most women worked their time in the laundry.

When prisons were nationalised in 1877, Wandsworth remained a short-term prison, but acquired a gallows: London was deemed to need two hanging prisons. Newgate (later Pentonville) continued its role in the north, and Wandsworth took over from Horsemonger Lane in the south.

In the first days of the Second World War a man who had been recruited as a German spy was obliged to transmit false messages from his Wandsworth cell. For this cooperation he was allowed to live, but several spies were later to be executed here.

Wormwood Scrubs

Unlike the other nineteenth-century prisons, Wormwood Scrubs was from the first a national rather than a local London prison. It was conceived as a national penitentiary for long-term prisoners, to replace the expensive Millbank failure, and the Prison Commissioners were determined to provide better and healthier accommodation. The radial plan was abandoned as too dark and gloomy: the blocks at the Scrubs were separate and parallel, built by convict labour guarded by ex-soldiers armed with rifles.

The use of Wormwood Scrubs soon changed – it became a local short-term prison, and contained one of the first Borstal units, giving training to young offenders.

During the Second World War the prison was for a time taken over as offices for Military Intelligence, and even provided a temporary home for a priceless hoard of heavy water. This was the rare material needed to control nuclear reactions, and the entire world supply, smuggled from France ahead of the advancing German armies, was brought to the prison for safe keeping.

It was from Wormwood Scrubs that the Soviet spy George Blake made his famous escape in 1966; sentenced to the longest fixed sentence ever passed by an English court – forty-two years imprisonment – Blake was sprung, not by the KGB, but by three amateurs.

THE ROAD TO TYBURN

All you that in the condemned hole do lie,
Prepare you, for tomorrow you shall die;
Watch all and pray; The hour is drawing near.
That you before the Almighty must appear.

Examine well yourselves; in time repent.
That you may not to eternal flames be sent.
And when St Sepulchre's Bell in the morning tolls
The Lord above have mercy on your souls.

At the western limits of all London, beyond the City and Westminster, in a field close to the meeting-point of three great roads, stood the Triple Tree. Three tall posts were set in a triangle and their tops joined by strong beams – this was for the gallows on which London put to death its criminals. This was Tyburn, and from those beams tens of thousands of men, women and children were hanged. The giant killing frame was not the first gallows to stand at Tyburn, nor the last, but for two hundred years it stood as the grimmest evidence of the English faith in capital punishment, serving a city which put to death more of its criminals than any other in the world.

This spot was first chosen for executions as early as the twelfth century – the road junction was a landmark easily found, and there was space enough for thousands to attend; perhaps there was at first a prominent tree from which felons could be strung up. To go so far beyond the capital also allowed the ceremony of a procession, a chance to parade the condemned and show that justice was being done and to give clear warning of the penalty for crime. The whole event took on the flavour of a public celebration, and was known ironically as a Tyburn Fair.

That road to Tyburn led from the Condemned Hold in Newgate, where many of the prisoners would have been held for weeks following their trial, beyond daylight and with great irons on their legs. On the day of execution the prisoners were led into the Press Room, where their irons were struck off, and a cord used to pinion their elbows behind their backs.

Most of the condemned would then be placed in carts, with a noose hung around each neck, and seated on their own coffins. For some of them, this last ride was an opportunity for a final flourish of showmanship, and they dressed in their finest clothes; others knew that the hangman would seize and sell their clothing, and chose a simple shift or nightshirt to rob the executioner of his profit. To protest his innocence to the last, many a man would dress in white or sport a white cockade.

A rich man might choose to ride to Tyburn in his own carriage, or hire one for the day; in carriage or cart, prisoners were often joined by family or friends for the last journey, to comfort them or share in the drinking. For traitors there was neither comfort nor company except a guard with drawn sword, as it was laid down that anyone convicted of treason must be dragged on a sledge or hurdle, scraping roughly across the ground through every kind of filth and mud, exposed to the anger of the crowd.

Whatever the transport, the first stage of the journey was marked by the ringing of a handbell outside St Sepulchre's, the church at the gates of the prison, and the bellman repeated the verse he had chanted the night before. The crowd would already be gathered waiting to follow the procession, and by custom young girls would throw posies or nosegays which prisoners might fasten to their clothes or carry as they rode.

The Ordinary – the prison chaplain – and the hangman would find places on the carts, and all would form a convoy, guarded by an escort under the command of the City Marshal: to hold back the crowds, and prevent any attempt at escape or rescue, he led a force of two hundred men.

Hanging days had a holiday atmosphere – to enjoy a Tyburn Fair the common people would leave their work and the curious gentry would form parties to see the execution as they might have arranged to enjoy a day at the races. Along every pace of the route were crowds eating and drinking, shouting and fighting. Stallholders and pedlars of all kinds sold their wares to the crowd, busking musicians and shouting showmen adding to a macabre carnival mood – 'All the Way, from Newgate to Tyburn is one continued fair, for Whores and Rogues of the meaner Sort.' Pickpockets and robbers relished the rich pickings to be made by cutting through so large a crowd, and street tricksters found easy victims among the drunk and unwary.

HALF-HANGED SMITH

On Christmas Eve 1705, the housebreaker John Smith had been hanging at Tyburn for fully a quarter of an hour when his reprieve arrived. The rope was cut, and Smith was still alive. He seems to have learned little from this narrow escape: twice more he stood trial on fresh capital charges, but his luck held – he was acquitted once, and was saved on the eve of this last trial by the sudden death of the prosecutor.

THE HANGING OF
EARL FERRERS
*Earl Ferrers was a violent
man, who cold-bloodedly
shot his steward through the
head. He was tried,
convicted and condemned
at a rare trial in the House
of Lords; Ferrers asked to
be beheaded, as he believed
fitting for a peer, but the
authorities insisted that he
hang as a common
murderer. Dressed in his
wedding suit, Ferrers
arrived in his own fine
carriage at Tyburn, where
he was the first man to be
hanged using a scaffold with
a trapdoor; his body was
then taken to Surgeons'
Hall for display and
dissection.*

On every side broadsheets were sold which claimed to report the last confessions of the prisoners about to die. By tradition this trade was a privileged sideline for the prison chaplains, who pursued prisoners for any juicy details – if the prisoner refused to play along, they simply made them up – and organised the printing and sale of thousands of copies. Sold at sixpence each, the handbills served much the same purpose as a theatre programme today, and yielded enormous profits in notorious cases.

The progress of the convoy through the crowd was always slow, as it made its way along what is now Oxford Street, and the journey might take as long as three hours to complete. When he was at the height of his power, Jonathan Wild would ride ahead of the carts, shouting to the crowd that his 'children' – those whom he was sending to their deaths – would soon be coming. It was usual for the carts to pause at a number of taverns along the route, where the prisoners would take a drink or two. The conventional joke for a prisoner was to call for a pint glass of brandy, with a promise that he would pay on his way back! The alcohol made prisoners bolder and if they were popular they made speeches during these stops, shook hands with the men and flirted with the girls,

but those whom the people hated were abused and manhandled, and every kind of missile, from dung and stones to dead animals, was hurled at them.

As the carts came closer to Tyburn the crowds were more and more tightly packed and impenetrable, and the last yards to the gallows were often the scene of a battle between the escort and the drunken mob in which dozens might be injured, even killed. At Tyburn itself there was a permanent theatre of death as sinister as any Roman arena. The Triple Tree itself stood at the centre, replacing earlier gallows which had been erected only for each hanging day, and around the tree there were high banks of benches like modern grandstands, to give those who had the price of a seat the best possible view of the executions. These stands were long owned by a widow called Proctor, who must have died rich – the rental of 'Mother Proctor's Pews' for the day of Lord Ferrers' execution in 1760 brought in £5000.

Around the grandstands were the horses and coaches of the well-heeled who had arrived earlier, now swamped as the mob which had followed the carts spilled around. Among the crowds and pushing forward to be close to the gallows might be men paid by families to seize the body after hanging, to take it away in the hope of reviving it or at least spiriting it away. There would often be friends of the condemned who wanted to give them comfort, and enemies who wanted to curse them and take pleasure in their deaths.

The events at the gallows could also be very long-winded. There could be many condemned – the full capacity of the gallows was twenty-four, and this number was reached at least once – each of whom might extend the wait by addressing the crowd, or taking time with the chaplain, or brawling with the hangman.

The crowd's tension would mount during any delay: it was not uncommon for a reprieve to arrive, or be announced, while the condemned were actually beneath the scaffold. If the life spared was a popular one, there would be riotous rejoicing, but a mob thirsty for blood could attack on the instant. The stands were demolished in 1758 during an outbreak which followed the reprieve of a man convicted of treason – the prolonged death of a traitor was a particular attraction. One unsavoury Ordinary, the Reverend Villette, was enraged when a reprieve arrived for a young boy wrongly sentenced to death for someone else's crime: the chaplain launched a furious attack on the hangman, telling him to make haste and hang the boy – it was too late

Lamentation and Execution
OF JAMES LONGHURST

At Horsemonger Lane Gaol, on Tuesday, April 16th, for the wilful murder of Jane Sax, a little Girl seven years old, at Shere, in Surrey.

Terrible Scene in the Prison with the Culprit.

James Longhurst, was executed this morning April 16, on the top of Horsemoner-lane gaol. Since his condemnation he has expressed contrition for his crime, and hoped that God would forgive him. Notwithstanding the prisoner appearing to be in a state of mind becoming his awful position, when he was taken down from the condemned cell to the yard to be pinioned a frightful scene ensued: The moment the culprit saw Calcraft, the executioner approach him with the straps to pinion his arms. he started back with an aspect of terror depicted on his countenance, and began to struggle violently with the turnkeys. The chaplain spoke to him and endeavoured to calm him, and this for a moment appeared to have the effect, but upon the executioner requesting that the culprit might be taken outside, as he could not see to fasten the straps properly, another fearful struggle ensued, and it required five warders to hold him, and it was necessary to throw him down and hold him on the ground while he was being pinioned, and one or two of the turnkeys were very much hurt by the kicks they received. The prisoner's conduct seemed to be actuated by an uncontrollable horror of the executioner and the apparatus of death. After he had been secured he walked quietly by the side of the chaplain until he arrived at the steps leading to the scaffold, and immediately he caught sight of the gibbet his horror appeared to return. He again struggled violently as well as he was able, and was forcibly dragged up to the steps and held under the beam by several turnkeys while the rope was adjusted round her neck, and as speedily as possible the bolt was drawn, and after a few struggles the wretch youth ceased to exist.

Good people all I pray draw near,
And my sad history you soon shall hear
And when the same I do relate,
I trust you will a warning take.

At Horsemonger-lane on the scaffold high,
For a cruel murder I was doomed to die

James Longhurst, it is my name,
I've brought myself to grief and shame,
Through the dreadful deed that I had done,
At Churchill-field, near Guildford town.

It was in last June, the twenty-eighth,
I did this deed as I now state;
An innocent child I there did slay,
And with a knife took her life away.

Poor Jane Sax, on that fatal day,—
A child scarce seven years of age;
In Churchill-field, I her did meet,
And shamefully did her illtreat.

Then coward-like I drew my knife,
To rob this helpless child of life;
I stabbed her in the throat—her blood did pour—
Then left her welt'ring in her gore.

Then I was taken for this cruel deed,
And sent for trial, as you may read;
At Kingston assizes, tried and cast,
Oh, would I could recall the past.

She cried for help did poor little Jane,
David Edsor to her assistance came;
Whilst I, a guilty wretch did stand,
And licked her blood from off my hand

The Judge said, James Longhurst you are guilty found,
You will go from here to London town
And there you'll die a detah of shame,
And meet your fate at Horsemonger-lane

While I lay in my prison cell,
My state of mind, no tongue can tell;
I could not rest by day or night,
Poor Jane was always in my sight.

My tender parents came to visit me,
My heart was breaking their grief to see
Tears from their eyes did in torrents fall
While for mercy to my God did call.

I hope that none will them upbraid,
While I am in my silent grave;
Farewell to all,—the bell does toll,
Have mercy, God, on my sinful soul.

H. Disley, Printer, 57, High Street, St. Giles, London.

HANDBILL FOR A HANGING

As each notable prisoner made his way to the gallows handbills were sold like programmes, detailing the crime and any confession or repentance. Most were fanciful, many were fictions, but they sold in their tens of thousands and yielded a rich income for the publishers and the authors, often prison chaplains who claimed to have had private and privileged access to the condemned cells.

now to waste time on such details! To the disappointment of the chaplain the boy's life was spared.

The original method of hanging had been to place the prisoner on a ladder, forcing him upwards and drawing him by the rope around his neck. Once high enough, many prisoners were brave or desperate enough to throw themselves off the ladder, hoping that the first shock would help them to a quick death. Those who could not bring themselves to make the leap were dislodged by the hangmen, who seized the ladder and 'turned them off' – an expression still used to describe execution.

When the Triple Tree went up, it was broad enough for a cart to drive beneath, and it became the practice simply to stand the prisoners at the cart's tail, place the thin nooses around their necks, and urge on the horses to draw the cart away. Death came by strangulation, and might take many minutes – to speed the end some prisoners flung themselves into the air, many were assisted by friends who rushed to haul on their legs or beat their chests.

Such slow and painful public dying arouses our pity and horror, but was then so commonplace that it was dismissed by the public: 'There is nothing in being hang'd but a wry Neck, and a wet pair of Breeches.' As for the deterrent effect, the intimidation which would put a stop to thieving – it was at the moment when the crowd was intent on watching a criminal being turned off that the many pickpockets in the crowd were able to work best.

The condemned themselves seem largely to have accepted their deaths very passively, though many may have become so very drunk by the time they reached Tyburn as to be beyond any sharp awareness of what was happening. Just a few were able to put up a formidable fight at the last minute, to the great entertainment of the crowd: Hannah Dagoe was one who managed to get her hands free to land a mighty punch on the hangman, then fling her clothes into the crowd so that he should see no profit from them. When at last they were able to put the noose around her neck, Dagoe threw herself from the cart with such force that the rope snapped. You had to go to a lot of hangings to find as much entertainment as that.

Those who were unafraid of death were often still frightened of the anatomists. The schools of surgery needed bodies which could be cut up by students of anatomy, but the ration of corpses permitted under law was too small to meet the demand, and a black market grew which encouraged grave-robbing and bodysnatching of all kinds. There was good money to be made from the trade in corpses, and what source could equal Tyburn as a supplier of fresh bodies? Some of the condemned men would sell their bodies in advance to raise money for their families, and hangmen were always ready to make cash deals, but there could also be thugs lurking ready by the gallows to snatch any unclaimed corpse by force.

There was an understandable squeamishness about dissection, and most of the condemned and their families took comfort in the prospect of a Christian burial, dreading the casual disposal that was given to the last portions of a dissected body. Most alarmed were any condemned whose faith helped them to face execution but who believed that if

NEWGATE HANGINGS 1809

When the shameful procession to Tyburn ended, most executions took place in the street outside Newgate prison, first using a primitive gallows at street level, and then on the new scaffold shown here, which used a trapdoor. On each hanging day, carpenters hammered together the wooden framework in the early morning, and draped it with black cloth as the crowds gathered.

they were not buried whole, they could not pass into an afterlife. The fearful of all kinds made plans to have themselves removed quickly by force or deception so that the bodysnatchers should not have them, and struggles over bodies could become so violent that further deaths resulted, and more culprits be condemned to hang.

As the prisoners died, the competition for their bodies began. From out of the crowd would push people who wanted to press the hands of the dead against their own infections or injury, believing the superstition that this would provide a cure. Worse, there were those who wanted to hack off portions of the body, hoping to take away a relic such as hands, hair or blood to bring good luck or a remedy. The same superstitions attached to the rope itself, and hangmen would sell short pieces to a clamouring crowd (the market was good enough for many hangmen to provide themselves with a great deal more rope than had in fact been used).

The authorities did not usually try to intervene at this stage; they were unconcerned about who got the corpses, but they had learned to be wary of attempts to bring hanged men back to life. Some of the friends who seemed to be putting their weight on a hanged man's legs might in truth be supporting him, and hangmen had often been bribed

THE MANNINGS ARE HANGED AT HORSEMONGER LANE GAOL (1849)
This is the crowd whose 'atrocious bearing looks and language' so repelled Dickens when he went to witness the hanging of the Mannings – Leech, the artist who joined him on that day, found the crowd more terrible than the hanging that took place on the prison roof high above.

HANGING IN SMITHFIELD

Not all the condemned made the journey to Tyburn. In the City portable gallows could be taken to the scene of a crime, or set up wherever the authorities chose to make an example of the prisoner. This was the execution of John Perrott, a bankrupt who was condemned because he hid much of his wealth from his creditors – a financial crime whose punishment was intended to warn other traders.

to contrive an arrangement of rope and knot that was unlikely to kill quickly.

Even without artificial help, some survived. Medical knowledge was limited and when the dying was so slow, it could be difficult to be certain that all life had gone – one man woke up as he lay in Surgeons' Hall, about to be dissected. Even these rare spontaneous cases encouraged attempts to resuscitate: Jack Sheppard's friends stood ready with blankets and a surgeon, but ironically were held at bay too long by a mob which thought they were bodysnatchers. When Dr Dodd was hanged a variety of treatments were tried without success.

After death, some bodies were hidden away by families, but some were carried back into town to lie in state in local houses or inns. Their friends who had been with them from prison to gallows now laid them out as the centrepieces for a rowdy wake, often drinking with money that the dead man had left for the purpose.

Tyburn was where common criminals were put to death, with none of the dignity of a grand state execution. After the Restoration it was the Cavaliers' revenge to dig up the bodies of Cromwell and two of his lieutenants, and carry them to Tyburn to swing at a rope's end. The heads were then cut off to be displayed on the roof of Westminster Hall, but the bodies were slung into a pit beneath the gallows, to lie in disgrace among all the countless unclaimed bodies of the friendless poor who had been buried without ceremony nearby.

From the middle of the eighteenth century enlightened opinion was turning against the bestiality of the Tyburn Fairs. A first step was the passing of the Murder Act of 1752, which ordered that the bodies of all murderers should be dissected and exposed to public view: this solved the surgeons' difficulties, eliminated the brawls with bodysnatchers, and increased the horror of a death sentence. Still Henry Fielding and other supporters of the Murder Act hoped for more. Horrified by the public brutalities of the hanging days, the vice and the violence, they campaigned for executions to be held swiftly and privately. Fielding's opinion was that 'The day appointed by law for a thief's shame is the day of glory in his own opinion' – low criminals were treated as heroes just when they should be reviled. A criminal should be executed while the public remembered his offence most sharply, and were unswayed by any sympathy or admiration for him as he passed through the streets. Hidden from view, hangings would become more sinister and horrifying in the popular imagination, and crime would become less glamorous.

Of course the traditionalists still believed that only public display would deter. They agreed with Doctor Johnson's response: 'Sir, executions are intended to draw spectators. If they do not draw spectators. they don't answer their purpose ... the public was gratified by a procession; the criminal was supported by it. Why is all this to be swept away?'

Change came, but slowly. After two hundred years of constant use, the Triple Tree was felled in 1759, its timbers sawn into props for the barrels of beer in a tavern close by. The substitute was to be a smaller, less dramatic portable gallows carried to the site with the condemned, and returned to storage after use. The first use of a scaffold with a trapdoor was at Tyburn, when Earl Ferrers was hanged for the murder of a servant, but the drop was too short and he had to be finished off 'by the pressure of the executioner'.

The Tyburn gallows stood close to the present Marble Arch, and it is quite impossible now to imagine the scenes that took place here week in, week out for close to six hundred years. To the hangings must be added the burnings of women, the dismembering of traitors, and the shooting of military offenders by firing squads close by in what is now Hyde Park: it is probable that sixty thousand Londoners were carried, dragged or driven here to die.

The squalid scenes along the route to the gallows, and the constant threat of riot, led to repeated demands for change, and the sheriffs were finally convinced that the brutal festivities must end, and the official place of execution be moved. Various sites were considered and dismissed because they would still require a procession, and the final choice was to conduct executions directly outside the walls of Newgate. 1783 saw the last hanging at Tyburn, and the first in front of the prison.

Though never as notorious as Tyburn, there had been another regular carnival for the bloodthirsty: south of the Thames, prisoners condemned at the Surrey courts were taken to Kennington Common for execution. There were brandy-sellers and pie-stalls, pickpockets and prostitutes, a debauched turmoil which drew tens of thousands. If both Tyburn and Kennington were to hold executions on the same day, sensation seekers had to consider carefully which event might offer the greater amusement.

THE HANGMEN

For eight hundred years and more, a hangman had a trade without honour, a job for the lowest and meanest of men who would not only execute prisoners, but carry out all the many chores of whipping, branding and mutilating, of dismembering traitors, even of burning books damned by the authorities. In France, and much of Germany, the public executioner held a post of public responsibility and was expected to perform his duties with dignity and skill – as did the man summoned from Calais to behead Anne Boleyn – but Londoners died at the hands of incompetents, drunks and criminals, men whose own lives commonly ended on the scaffold.

The earliest executioner on record, the man who beheaded the Duke of Northumberland in 1553, was described only by his stump leg, and we can identify just a few of his successors. Derrick is recalled in the name given to a type of crane; this has suggested to some that he used to winch up his victims, but it is probably just an ironic play on words. Derrick himself was a vicious man who was condemned for rape, but reprieved at the request of the Earl of Essex – it is ironic that the hangman survived to behead Essex some years later. Dickens included a character called Ned Dennis in *Barnaby Rudge*, and there was a real-life Edward Dennis – a hangman who was condemned to death for his part in the Gordon Riots. As he waited to hang, he asked that his son should succeed him; the authorities seemed to flinch at the idea of son hanging father, so Dennis was pardoned to execute thirty-four of his fellow rioters.

The most famous name of all was that of Jack Ketch, himself a rapist and murderer, who methodically put to death more than two hundred of Monmouth's rebel followers, then messily beheaded the Duke himself. Ketch's notoriety was such that the public gave his name to many of his successors, including the despicable John Price, a pickpocket and petty thief who was recruited as the Middlesex hangman, but was himself executed in 1718 after he had drunkenly beaten a woman to death.

Hypocritically, the public loved a hanging but detested the hangman, and were always ready to attack an executioner who carried out his task sloppily. They knew that in addition to the fee, the executioner would steal anything from a body, even the body itself, and take extra profit selling pieces of the rope, locks of hair, and any supposedly magical memento of the dead.

The crude chores of an old hanging or burning, even the elaborate slaughter of a traitor, demanded a strong stomach but nothing by way of skill. It was the use of a drop, a scaffold with trapdoors, which called for some craftsmanship in rigging and operating the mechanism, but the first practitioners made no attempt to use the new gallows mercifully. The most famous of the nineteenth-century hangmen, who served for forty-five years, was Calcraft, whose caperings on the scaffold were an affront to Victorian high seriousness. Dickens tartly wrote that 'Mr

CALCRAFT USES THE WHIP
Hangmen were paid to carry out floggings: the most famous of Victorian executioners was Calcraft, who retired at the age of seventy-three after forty-five years of mediocre service. His manners were coarse, he was sometimes the worse for drink, and his methods were notoriously slow and inhumane.

Calcraft, [who] should be restrained in his unseemly briskness, in his jokes, his oaths and his brandy.' Worse, Calcraft was incompetent, using too short a rope to ensure a swift death, and commonly reduced to leaping onto the backs of his victims, or heaving at their legs, to shorten their agony.

It was Calcraft's more dignified successor, Marwood, who first used an understanding of weights and drops to calculate the length of rope which would ensure a merciful death for a particular victim, setting standards which others were obliged to observe. When executions were conducted in the street, the main concern of the authorities had been to maintain order, but at the more solemn private hangings they required reliability, discretion and skill. Obliged to watch each hanging at close quarters, it is easy to imagine why a sheriff would wish to hire an executioner who worked with dignity and efficiency.

In the end, the Home Office imposed strict codes, ensured that only approved hangmen could be employed, and required a report on their performance to be submitted after each execution. Into the strange closed fraternity of official killers came a wide variety of odd and unsuitable personalities, but it also included some who followed a family tradition, and several who took an honest pride in performing their work humanely, like Albert Pierrepoint, who followed his uncle and father into the calling but concluded that capital punishment was a worthless act of revenge.

FINDING OUT MORE

Visitors and Londoners alike will find evidence of London's sinister past all about them. Crowds still emerge from the dungeons of the Tower to stand on Tower Green and recall the solemn and pitiable deaths of Queens. Taxi drivers point out to their passengers the site of Tyburn Triple Tree at Marble Arch, tourists in Whitehall still pause at the spot where a king was beheaded.

The buildings of the City may be modern glass and steel, but they follow a pattern of streets set down many hundreds of years ago, and it is easy to imagine, strolling with one of the knowledgeable guides who lead regular tours, the ancient maze of alleys held tight within the City walls, the prowling footpads and bursting riots.

This book has been the broadest introduction to our capital's crimes and bloodthirsty ways. You may wish to learn more, or to explore the streets to see for yourself some of the less famous criminal landmarks – the stable in Cato Street where the conspirators were captured still stands, and just outside the Tate Gallery is the spot from which many thousands of convicts were transported to the far side of the world.

Martin Fido's *Murder Guide to London* is one of several intriguing street-by-street books about specific murders in the past: Donald Rumbelow's *The Triple Tree* goes further back to draw vivid links between Newgate, the Old Bailey and Tyburn; Philip Collins' *Dickens and Crime* sets out in great detail the novelist's researches into Victorian crime and punishment; and though it is only indirectly concerned with the crimes, my own *Prisons and Punishments of London* gives a detailed account of London's treatment of its criminals.

Acknowledgements

Pictures

British Library – pages 40, 41

Mary Evans Picture Library – pages 14, 16, 20, 21, 26, 28, 29, 30, 46, 49, 54, 57, 59, 60, 62, 120, 151, 173, 206, 213, 232, 234

John Frost Collection – page 123

National Portrait gallery, Syndication International – pages 130, 131, 137, 138, 139, 140, 142.

The remainder are from the author's collection.

My thanks to Alice Wood, Martin Bryant, Andrew Lownie, Martin Baggoley, Don Robinson, Heather French and Sue Ryall for the parts they have played in the making of this book.

Little, Brown now offers an exciting range of quality titles by both established and new authors. All of the books in this series are available by faxing, or posting your order to:

Little, Brown and Company (UK) Limited
Mail order,
P.O. Box 11,
Falmouth,
Cornwall, TR10 9EN
Fax: 0326-376423

Payments can be made as follows: Cheque, postal order (payable to Little, Brown Cash Sales) or by credit cards, Visa/Access/Mastercard. Do not send cash or currency. U.K.customers and B.F.P.O.; Allow £1.00 for postage and packing for the first book, plus 50p for the second book, plus 30p for each additional book up to a maximum charge of £3.00 (7 books plus) U.K. orders over £75 free postage and packing.

Overseas customers including Ireland, please allow £2.00 for postage and packing for the first book, plus £1.00 for the second book, plus 50p for each additional book.

NAME (Block Letters)

....

ADDRESS

....

....

....

☐ I enclose my remittance for ....

☐ I wish to pay by Visa/Access/Mastercard

Number ☐☐☐☐☐☐☐☐☐☐☐☐☐☐☐

Card Expiry Date ☐☐☐☐

Unlock the darkest secrets of the Dungeon.

Dare you discover what terrors lie in wait behind the doors of the world's most infamous museum of horror?

Buried beneath London Bridge Station, Tooley Street SE1. Unlocked from 10 am every day including Sundays.

A perfectly horrible experience.

the london Dungeon

Special Offer

TWO TICKETS FOR THE PRICE OF ONE
to visit the world famous
LONDON DUNGEON

When you visit the London Dungeon and pay the full adult entrance fee, you will be able to take another adult with you – completely *free of charge*. Please complete this voucher and send it to:

London Dungeon Ticket Offer, Special Sales Dept.,
Little, Brown and Company (UK) Ltd,
165 Great Dover Street, London SE1 4YA

Name _____

Address _____

_____

_____ Postcode _____

This offer closes on 1st June 1994.
One voucher per person.
Not to be used in conjunction with any other offer.

FOR OPENING TIMES, PRICES ETC. PLEASE CALL
THE LONDON DUNGEON INFORMATION LINE
ON 071-403 0606